A House Reconciled

Journeying Through My Parents' Divorce

Caitlyn Neel

ACKNOWLEDGEMENT

A special thank you to:

Marian Raney, Editor

Rebecca Noll, Cover Artist

CONTENTS

PREFACE

You're not alone in this thing. I am with you. I am for you.
Whether your parents are divorced or currently in the
process, I want you to know that this book is for you. I
don't completely understand your pain or your
circumstance. Everyone's story is different. Yet maybe
my story can intersect with your story just enough to
bring you a little hope.

When I was a teenager, my parents got a divorce. No
one really knew what to say or how to help me. There
weren't any books that guided me through a healing
process.

Today, I know so many students with divorced
parents that it breaks my heart. So, I've compiled a series
of memories and lessons I've learned over the years into
this book to encourage those students and you. It's also
possible that you're a parent or friend who's trying to
better understand what it's like for a kid in this situation.
Hopefully my experiences in this book will give you the
insight for which you're searching.

The first half of this book is predominantly my
experience reacting to my parents getting a divorce. We'll
relive my middle and high school years while I come to
terms with this big change in my life.

Once I was in college, my heart finally began to heal.
The second half of the book will explore my journey of
overcoming fear, allowing myself to process the pain, and
healing broken relationships.

This book in your hand is my heart. I've completely opened up to you. Here I am. Here's my story. This is the real me. My tears, my hopes, my dreams. It's been a journey of brokenness and healing. I'm opening my heart to you and letting you see deep inside. Please be gentle with me and breathe in the truth that I've discovered along the way.

At the end of each chapter, I'll give you some direction to help you connect my experiences to your story. For those of you whose parents are not divorced or not currently going through a divorce, you can probably skip over this part. But for those of you who are, you will be presented with opportunities to open your own heart and sift through what's inside. Reading this book won't be easy, but as you experience this hope, it will bring healing into your life.

Consider inviting someone to walk with you through this book. Doing life together, especially the messy parts, is much better than doing it alone. This will be difficult, but even so, keep going. Don't stop. Don't give up.

Okay. Are you ready? Let's begin the journey.

1 NOT SO PERFECT

I found a picture. Not just any picture, but a picture of my old house. Or should I say my old home. This was the place where countless memories were made.

My house was the white one with blue shutters. There was a front screened-in porch with a squeaky swing. The piano in the foyer, played by many, frequently filled the house with wonderful music. A dartboard graced the basement wall with a ceiling full of little holes, clear evidence of our mad skills.

In the big backyard, we would jump in giant piles of colorful leaves in the fall, build snowmen in the winter, and plant flowers in the spring. In the summer as a little kid, I would dig into the dirt, add water and mix in grass, and serve my imaginary friend mud stew. I would play fetch with our dogs, Frisbee™ with my big brother Chris, and catch with my dad.

There was a secret room that could be accessed from

my bedroom closet. My dad and I built it and stored canned foods and keepsakes in there ... just in case. I would sneak in, peer through the vent, and spy on whoever was in the kitchen. When my dad and I weren't going on secret agent missions, we would play "Cowboys and Indians" or G.I. Joes™ with toys from my dad's childhood.

My mom would tuck me in at night and make up beautiful and exciting bedtime stories about King Redwood and his daughters Willow, Maple, and Magnolia. They were always embarking on some grand adventure, learning life lessons, or rescuing some hurt or lost animal.

Some days my older sister Carolyn and I would play with our Barbie™ dolls, dreaming up elaborate stories of how Barbie would marry Ken. Other days Chris would help me build LEGO™ ships that would explore the vast universe and shoot down enemy war crafts with hi-tech lasers. But even better were the epic "sock wars." While Carolyn and I wore Chris' jackets as armor, the three of us would take my brother's socks, stuffing one inside the other, and pelt each other with them.

As a family, the five of us played games together and went on makeshift explorations. One time we gathered together our ropes and clips and made the difficult climb up the massive mountain. Well, okay, so it was just our staircase that led up to the second floor, but to the imagination of a five-year-old, it sure felt like a mountain. Another time we pretended empty milk jugs were oxygen tanks and our basement a cave where we went spelunking.

For the Fourth of July, we entered an elaborate float into the town's big parade. The theme was "Picnic in the Park" so we covered our Dodge Intrepid in red and white checkered picnic tablecloths and filled the open trunk with large fruit, which we constructed out of cloth, wires, and cartoon faces. I then pinned green and purple balloons to my green shirt and sat in the trunk as a bunch of grapes, waving to everyone watching the parade. On top of the car, we built a grill with a giant hotdog. As we drove down the street, my mom would light a smoke bomb and stick it through the sunroof so that the grill would smoke as it "cooked" the hotdog.

We were also in the town's annual cardboard boat regatta. CJ's Family Tree was the name of our boat because we built a giant cardboard tree on top. Occasionally, we would go on a camping trip during the summer. Now, not all these trips were perfect, but they did make for some comical memories. Like the RV trip where everything went wrong, and we literally had to stop at a mechanic daily.

My siblings and I played park district sports, took up musical instruments, and dabbled in the arts. We would faithfully attend church twice a week and do all sorts of fun family activities together.

Yes. I had the perfect family. Or so I believed.

The Broken Reality

Slowly I began to realize I had been totally clueless that my entire world wasn't so perfect. It turned out that many times our family's persona of perfection was only a mask covering up the messy truth.

A couple weeks before I started sixth grade, my mom moved all her things from my parents' room upstairs down into the basement bedroom. I didn't quite understand the horrible implications of this new reality until a friend came to visit. We were hanging out and decided to watch a movie so we went downstairs to the family room in the basement. Just before we hit the power button on the TV, my mom walked past and into the bedroom, closing the door behind her.

"Where's your mom going?" My friend asked in innocence.

"Her bedroom," I replied nonchalantly.

"Your mom lives down here?"

The tone of her voice radically opened my eyes to the dark reality of my family's brokenness.

"Oh," I was completely dumbfounded, and my heart sank.

Somehow my family wasn't so perfect. Looking back, I now realize I had ignored all the problems that had plagued my family. I'm not just talking about the times my siblings ganged up on me or the dog peed on the carpet; I'm talking about the times I would sit at the top of the stairs, listening to my parents arguing in the living room, screaming back and forth at each other. I'm talking about the Sunday afternoon when my parents were having a heated argument in the dining room while I ate my chicken noodle soup and grilled cheese sandwich. My dad was fuming.

"You're scaring Cait," my mom told him. I just sat there and watched, apathetic to the whole scene. Frantically my mom picked up her purse and told me to come with her. My dad grabbed her purse and cried out for her not to leave. She told him she would come back, and he let go reluctantly.

My mom and I went to the park. She immediately dialed our church to speak with the pastor-on-call and asked what to do. Things were bad. Yet, I couldn't accept it; I was completely dead to this new reality. The sensitivity I once had as a little girl was drifting away. None of this nightmare was real. I mean, the idea of divorce never crossed my mind. Not in *my* family. It wasn't even an option.

Breaking the News

It was a beautiful, sunny afternoon. My parents sat us three kids down in our family room to talk. I can picture the scene clearly in my mind as if it was yesterday. My sister sat to my right and my brother next to her. My dad sat across from me with my mom to his left. I was light-hearted and joyful, wondering what new adventure my family would embark on next.

My dad looked us in the eyes and announced, "Mom and I are getting divorced."

I laughed.

Yes. I'm serious. I laughed. This experience was so surreal that I laughed.

It was even traumatic enough that apparently, my brain remembered things completely different than how that day really occurred. That clear picture in my memory of my sister and brother sitting to my right and my parents across from us, I recently discovered, was wrong. We were upstairs in the living room, not the family room in the basement. And I was sitting next to my mom with my sister across from me. I wonder if I must have felt so strongly that the divorce was creating a division between my family, that my subconscious made me believe that there was a clear divide between my parents and us kids. I don't know.

What I do know is I do remember correctly that I laughed and when I laughed, my sister glared at me. Her sharp glare burned deep into my memory. And at that moment, for the first time, I realized this was serious. It wasn't some outrageous joke; it was real. My smile immediately dropped while my stomach started to turn in such a gut-wrenching pain that I had to gasp for air. It felt like my entire world suddenly halted to a dead stop.

Why Me

As a middle school student, I didn't know anyone with divorced parents. No one seemed to be going through the same experiences. I didn't know what to do or where to go. I began noticing the problems, but my mind couldn't grasp the significance and that this was really happening to me. You know how we hear stories about natural disasters or fatal car accidents, yet we never realize that could be us. Sure, people were getting divorced around me, but that would never touch my family. It was impossible.

I guess I was so used to my family arguing that I didn't realize it wasn't normal or okay. Later in life I learned that my parents sheltered me from a lot of what was really going on. So, from my perspective I just didn't get it. Why were my parents getting a divorce?

One day I found out that my friend's parents had almost gotten a divorce. I was surprised; I hadn't known that about her family. But thankfully, at the time, they had been able to work things out. So why couldn't my parents? Why could things not be fixed? It didn't make sense to me.

Why couldn't they forgive and fight for the relationship? It wasn't just their marriage they were ending; it was our whole family. I had so many questions of why and how and what now, most of which were never answered. Yet amid my confusion and ignorance, the problems in my family were surfacing and being unveiled for the world to see.

Unmasked Self

The truth had been revealed. The perfect image of my family was obliterated. A lot of people may have wondered how a loving God could allow divorce and so much pain to enter a person's life; you probably have wondered too. But God isn't some cruel god, unmasking people's deepest, darkest secrets for some sick, perverted pleasure, but rather it is through exposing the truth that we are set free. I didn't realize this at the time, and I still have a hard time believing it, but somehow, amid the confusion and pain, the crushing truth of the brokenness of our family was allowing each one of us to begin a journey of healing.

A few years ago, I started mentoring a group of high school freshmen girls. On Sunday afternoons during small group time, one girl enjoyed talking, laughing, and joking around, using her incredible talent to somehow change the discussion topic every couple of minutes from Jesus to SpongeBob™ or Pokémon™. At youth retreats, while the other girls shared the struggles in their lives, she tended to be quiet, listening, focusing on the others, while trying to avoid anyone noticing the problems she had in her own life.

As I spent more time with her, I quickly realized that her continuous happy demeanor was just her acting, which I must say, she was good at, especially onstage. But when I looked into her eyes, I could see the truth behind her low-key smile. I could see past the mask she put on for others, and I called her out on it. Without hesitation, she admitted to me that she was putting on a show. To my surprise, she then simply shrugged and walked away. She chose to wear that mask, and she wasn't going to do anything about it.

I'm guilty of the same thing, putting on a poker face, and not letting my weaknesses or imperfections show. There are so many stereotypes and expectations that we feel like society, family, friends, and even total strangers put on us. Growing up, my dad called us kids "geniuses" so I felt like I had to be successful and needed to reach ... well, perfection. I was "supposed" to attend college, graduate with honors, and get a high-paying, full-time job. Sometimes I felt pressure to be the "perfect" role model for all the teenagers I mentor. I was "supposed" to get married, have kids, and live in the typical American white house with blue shutters in the suburbs. I was expected to attend certain parties and have fun. If I didn't laugh at my dad's jokes, I'm told I'm too uptight and need to loosen up.

But here's the thing: I'm not perfect. Yet I try to be. I try to be the perfect friend, mentor, student, employee, the perfect daughter. But that's not who I'm meant to be. God knows I'm not perfect. He knows you're not perfect. He knows you inside and out, including even the dark, shadowy corners you deny even exist. And he loves you - the real you. With all the good *and* bad. That's why in Luke 12 Jesus warned his disciples of hypocrisy while encouraging them not to be afraid of what people think. God doesn't expect us to be perfect. He doesn't expect you to be perfect. God doesn't even want us striving to be some perfect person, especially when perfection tends to be defined more by culture and tradition than him. He simply wants us not to worry about what the world may think, and instead to be genuine and authentic, to be ourselves.

Well, time went by and the girl in my small group still wasn't being real. She ended up telling the small group about how her parents had filed for a divorce among other crappy things that were going on in her life, but she wouldn't show how it was affecting her. Finally, a year and a half later, around the time of the winter youth retreat, things suddenly changed. She finally began to let her real self show.

These were the words she used to describe what it felt like to be unmasked:

> "When you're wearing a mask in life, it's like you don't trust anyone. You just go throwing lies around because you're too afraid to let anyone see how you really feel. But when you're close enough to someone, or comfortable enough to take the mask off, it's liberating. It's hard to keep everything bottled in and just put on a face, and when you have someone you can be yourself around, it's such a free feeling."

She finally felt free to be herself and let us in. There was a total transformation. A year later, she and I were driving to church one day, and I asked her how she was really doing. Throughout that past year she had gone through some things no teen should ever have to go through. I was amazed at how completely honest she was with me. She freely admitted the pain in her life and how she was working through it.

Not too long ago, my mentor Bekah called me out on the very same thing. The two of us would meet for breakfast once a week and after the first few meetings she confronted me. I was leaning back in my chair with my arms crossed when she began pointing out how I was disrespecting her, not really caring about our meetings, and not letting her in. How could we talk about life when I wouldn't let her anywhere near my heart?

I was completely blown away. I had huge walls built up, and I wasn't letting her get to know me beyond the surface. My heart broke, when I realized what I had done. She gave me some time to think, and I quickly realized I wanted to change. I needed a mentor who would inspire me in my walk with God and was willing to love me enough to call me out on things in my life about which I was totally clueless. I needed someone who would walk alongside of me as I continued to heal from my past and move into the freedom Christ calls us. When we finally throw the mask aside and face the truth, healing takes place.

Questions to Explore

- What's your story? Write down what your family was like before your parents announced they were getting divorced.
- Do you remember how you found out your parents were getting a divorced? What happened?
- My mentor Bekah is several years older than me and was there to listen and walk with me through my struggles. Think of an adult with whom you can be open and honest, even if it's not easy. Write down their name.

2 LETTING THEM IN

I looked around the empty lobby, waiting for my dad to finish his conversation. Each second seemed agonizing. Pushing the door open, I stepped outside into the muggy air. I wiped my short, brown hair out of my face and dusted off my jean shorts and wrinkled white t-shirt, which had a picture of a dog on it.

It was a hot Wednesday night at the beginning of summer with the moon glowing through the foggy clouds. I walked across the parking lot away from my church toward our family van. My glasses hid the tears swelling up in my eyes. That Sunday I was supposed to graduate to the junior high youth group.

My family had been going to Calvary Church since before I was born. A lot of people knew me, mainly because of my parents' leadership within the church, but I didn't really know them. I was quiet and reserved, and my family lived too far from the church to have any type of play dates outside of Sunday morning or Wednesday night services. I had friends at school, but the only friend I had at church was Hilary, whom I've been friends with pretty much since the day she was born.

I would go over to her house for fun slumber parties, play card games, watch movies, and go swimming. At my house, we would play intense and almost deadly games of air hockey where the puck would become more like a dodgeball, shooting off the table directly toward our heads. Hilary's clearly professional dart throwing skills left dozens of little holes around the dartboard and even in the ceiling (ok, ok, I'm guilty of it too). And then there were the times we would play with my Nerf™ guns or make a sad attempt of playing tennis at the park across the street.

But there was a problem. Hilary's a year younger than me so this year I had to venture from the children's ministry program, where we always sat together, to the junior high service where, well, I felt completely alone. Picture this: I enter a room of 70 junior high students. I know their names, and they know mine; after all, we've grown up together. But the only person who greets me is a leader. Week after week I sit, alone, in the same isolated chair and try to look occupied by rereading the small news flyer about 15 times, waiting, counting down the agonizing minutes until the worship band finally starts. All I wanted was to feel like I belonged. But all I seemed to be able to do was disappear into the crowd and hide. I dreaded going every single Sunday and Wednesday. Sometimes I spent the car ride home hiding in the back seat, hoping no one would notice I was crying.

The only way I had survived Wednesday nights up until 6th grade was because my mom was one of the teachers and talking with her helped me to ignore the fact that I didn't have any friends. I had always liked the pastors and other leaders too, but that wasn't enough. I couldn't do it any longer. I started begging my parents to find a new church so I could start over, a church that was closer to home so I'd at least have a chance of making friends.

I needed to find a place where I belonged. Whether our lives are filled with lots of friends or loneliness, we all have a deep-rooted need for close friendship.

The D-Team

One day my dad told me he was praying that through the midst of the craziness at home, I'd have a solid group of friends in which to confide. My dad's prayer for me must have been answered because things suddenly changed in 7th grade. A year before the divorce was announced, one of the junior high youth group leaders invited me to join the "D-Team" she was forming. I was no longer going to be a loner, sitting in a dark corner yearning for a place to fit in and belong; I was going to have the thing I needed so much: a solid group of friends.

The "D" stands for discipleship. Basically "D-Team" was a fancy name for a small group of friends who would encourage each other in their relationships with God. The leader asked five 7th grade girls to join, and we all said yes. At the beginning, we were all kind of nervous, excited, and ... well ... awkward.

One Sunday afternoon, I hung out for the first time with Jennifer, one of the "D-Team" girls. I was dropped off at her house, and she led me into a cozy room with a TV and futon. We sat there in silence for a minute, not really knowing what to say. We asked each other a few dumb little questions that could only manage a short lame answer. Jennifer then dug into a cabinet and retrieved a board game. We played pretty much in silence.

Frankly, I thought she was weird, and it turns out that she was thinking the same thing about me. Well, as time went by, my friendship with Jennifer and the other girls got a whole lot better. We started having ridiculous sleepovers with epic games of Truth or Dare. Thus, we ended up eating some crazy concoctions including ingredients like peanut butter, hot chocolate powder, and pickles we snuck from the basement pantry. At one point, I remember Danielle trying to catch fish from the fish tank with her bare hand. We also stumbled upon some super old, cheesy aerobic workout videos buried deep within some closet.

We would go ice-skating together, go to Danielle's volleyball games, and even played basketball with our dads. We all went to different schools, but within a couple months we were best friends. Now I looked forward to going to church on Wednesday nights. Picture this: I enter a room of the same 70 junior highers. I know their names, and they know mine; after all, we've grown up together. And suddenly I hear my name. I gaze across the room as a couple of my new friends run over to say hi. I sit with them in the same row every week. We ask each other all sorts of questions, talking quickly, trying to get in as many stories as possible while the clock counts down the priceless minutes before the worship band starts.

I was no longer alone.

Being Me

Now I was surrounded by a solid group of friends who loved me for who I was. They constantly encouraged me to make good choices. For example, whenever we discussed boys, which was quite often, Stephanie would talk about how she wanted to save her first kiss for the man she planned to marry. She was convinced she would marry someone who was worth waiting for. Stephanie is now married, and the only man she ever kissed is her husband. I respect that.

You may experience peer pressure toward promiscuity. The possibility of absent parents doesn't help. But we are worth so much more than that. It's super important to know our standards and what our boundaries are before dating so we don't cross physical (and emotional, spiritual, social) lines we didn't intend to cross. Otherwise we might end up in difficult life-altering circumstances. So I decided to hold to high standards when it came to guys.

My D-Team also encouraged me in my relationship with God. As a group, we went to "The Core," a monthly junior high worship night at my church. We would sing worship songs together and pray for each other. One night we were praying together, and Danielle kept reminding us to "pray in the name of Jesus because the name of Jesus is powerful!" Her excitement to see Jesus answer our prayers rubbed off on me.

One Wednesday night we were standing together singing worship songs with our eyes closed and hands raised, which is a common posture. I looked at Stephanie next to me and saw her smiling ear-to-ear, so happy to be praising God for how incredibly good he is. It kind of shocked me. I was used to seeing people not smiling when worshiping God because it was supposed to be a serious thing. But in that moment, I realized worshiping God can be one of the most joyful things we do.

I learned a lot from this group of girls. Their encouraging words and simple presence in my life set my passion for God on fire. We constantly inspired each other to grow deeper in our walks with God. And their continued prayers for my family and me made me feel loved.

It was through their friendship that I learned I could be myself and that I was loved. I couldn't earn it or force it. I didn't do anything to make them be my friends. Our leader basically gave them to me. And there was nothing that I could do or say that would make them not accept me anymore. It was through them that I realized God's love for me. It was through their acceptance that I realized that God would never reject me but liked me just as I was. I couldn't make God like me by anything I said or did. He loved me simply because he is love.

In his perfect timing, God placed these girls in my life to help me through the divorce. In the safety of their friendship, I could endure the realities of my broken family. This new support system was crucial. If it wasn't for them and our leader, I don't know where I would have ended up.

An Open Book

I have a very hard time opening up and communicating my feelings. Unless someone specifically asks me a question about what's going on inside of me, I tend not to share.

One year, Stephanie gave me a birthday present. It was a Sunday morning in September, and we were in the large garage at the back of the church property where the youth group met while the building was under construction. The service had ended, and the two of us were standing in the middle of a couple hundred now-vacant, metal folding chairs.

She handed me what looked like a small gift-wrapped book. With intrigue, I tore off the paper and held the book *The Presence of Peace* tightly in my hands. It was a book full of the promises of God and encouraging Bible verses and quotes.

"I don't really understand what you're going through," Stephanie spoke gently. It was clear she was referring to my parents' divorce. "And I have no idea how to help. But I'm here for you, if you ever need anything."

Knowing I had a healthy group of friends who loved me and supported me made such a powerful impression on my life and provided me with encouragement and inspiration. Looking back, however, I realize that my friends could only be there for me to a very limited extent because I was still rather closed off to them. If I had let Stephanie in more, allowed her to see my pain and know my heart-felt longings and needs, she would have better understood and have had an idea of how to help.

By opening up to a trustworthy friend, more healing could have taken place, but I didn't. Fearful of what people may think when they saw the ugly mess within me, it was easier to box up my emotions, put on a poker face, and not let them in. It was a protection mechanism. I didn't want people to see my weakness and vulnerability for fear of being hurt even more. I had a fear of rejection.

Thus, I didn't let others really know me, and I certainly didn't go out of my way to get to know others. By trying to protect myself from others' rejection, I end up rejecting them. When I put walls up and I'm not sharing with the trustworthy people God has placed in my life, I'm not letting them love me nor am I showing them love. And that's our deepest desire: to be loved.

There are people who really do care about you and love you, yet we don't always let them because we are afraid to let them in, know us, and truly love us. But it doesn't have to be this way.

Being Known

So what does it mean when someone really knows you? I'm not talking about the superficial, surface-y stuff, but the real, know the good and the bad, seeing the things people try so hard to hide. When someone really knows you, and likes you despite it, that's love. When you don't have to earn acceptance, and there isn't anything you could do or not do to make someone love you, that's unconditional love. Once you have that support group, it's time to open up and let them in.

Shortly after my parents announced the divorce, Danielle noticed something had changed in me. She asked me what was wrong; I hesitated.

"Just trust me," I remember Danielle saying to me. Trust her? It seemed like a crazy idea to just trust her with the big news, but I was like, why not? So I decided to open up and let her in, and I'm glad I did.

It's a choice. It may be one of the hardest things to do, but it's possible. I can allow others to know me. A couple years ago, the person who I feared rejection from the most was my mentor Bekah. She understood me and was there for me, bringing the best out of me and helping me work through the worst. Yet, what if she just suddenly threw me to the curb and abandoned me? I felt like I had little to nothing to offer her; nothing I could do would ensure that she wouldn't reject me.

I woke up one morning with the realization of how this fear was affecting me and hurting my relationships. I drove to Bekah's apartment in tears. I walked up the stairs and stood in front of her screen door. I could see their puppy inside, cocking her head at me as if she was asking if I was going to come in. But I just stood there. I could see other people inside, and I didn't want to be a burden. I was vulnerable and was afraid to discover the answer to my haunting questions: Am I worth her time? Am I worth her stopping what she was doing with these other people to spend a few minutes with me?

Her husband noticed me at the front door, said hi, and called to Bekah for me. Immediately she came out, smiling, happy to see me. As soon as she realized I was upset, her entire countenance changed. Her smile dropped in concern, and she quickly wrapped me up in her arms.

We stood outside talking for a while. I opened up and shared with her what I was struggling with, admitting to her all my pain and fear. My body literally shook as I stood there because of my vulnerability as I let her see deep into my aching heart. She listened intently; everything else around us faded away. There was so much light in her eyes and the longer she talked with me, the more I felt loved and reassured.

Sometimes it's so hard to open up like that. One time it was so hard letting Bekah in on the truth of what I felt about myself that I literally couldn't get the words out of my mouth. So I wrote them down and handed the paper to her.

But even though it's hard to let someone see the real you and love on you, it's worth it. You're worth it. You are worth getting to know.

Questions to Explore

- Describe your friends. How do they influence you?

- Many church youth groups offer small groups like the one I had. Are you involved in a church youth group? If not, would you consider trying one?
- Remember the name you wrote down at the end of Chapter 1; you know, that adult you can trust? Reach out to that person. You'll probably feel vulnerable like I did, but it'll be worth it knowing someone has your back.

3 BRING IT ON

The air was crisp and cool. I looked up at the sky filled with stars. Sometimes living in the suburbs with all the streetlights made it difficult to see the stars, but not this night.

Usually I would sit inside on the top staircase landing, listening to my parents argue downstairs. I tended to have a curiosity for understanding my family and each person's pain, hoping that I would somehow be able to help fix the problem. I didn't realize at the time I was taking on burdens and responsibilities that a child never should have carried.

But this night, I needed some fresh air. There I was, standing on the back porch of my home. I tried to block out the yelling I could still hear coming from deep within the house. Slowly I sat down on the blue wooden steps. I took a deep breath. Something about the big oak trees and flashing fireflies gave me a sense of peace.

There was a rustling sound underneath me. My beautiful pure bread beagle Carmen emerged from beneath the back porch with her nose covered in dirt. I couldn't help but smile.

Suddenly, the screen door swung open behind me. It slammed shut and my sister Carolyn sat down next to me. I looked at her.

"How is this not affecting you?" I remember her asking. I could hear the pain in her voice and words.

My heart sank.

"It is," I replied quietly.

I guess all some people saw were my innocent smiles and optimistic joy. But deep down the divorce was changing everything.

Everything within me ached for something more, for purpose. I tried whatever my little self could do to make things better, but it was all in vain. One time I typed an anonymous letter to my dad, urging him to fight for the marriage and not get divorced. I addressed it to him, left the sender's information vacant, put a stamp on it, and secretly slipped it into the mailbox where he found it later that day. Yet all my attempts failed, and my struggle to fight for my own family ended in defeat.

The storm was too great for anything I could do or say. I was totally and completely helpless and weak. I needed faith in something greater than this disaster. I needed something that would somehow justify the divorce. As my whole world came crashing down and the things I once believed as true were shattered, I longed for something to hold onto, something that would stand firm as everything else fell apart. I needed a reason to live. I needed hope.

Broken Promise

Every summer my mom would purchase several cartons of colorful flowers from the elementary school annual sale, and we would plant them in a dirt patch right next to the back porch. And every summer those flowers would be neglected and die. My mom had good intentions, but frankly lacked a green thumb. In fact, nearly every plant she tried to care for would end up brown and droopy. It's true; even she admits it.

Well, one sunny afternoon I was outside and I noticed the abandoned flowers struggling to survive in the dry cracked earth. Taking pity on the poor plants, I turned to retrieve the watering can from the garage. But then I stopped. An idea popped into my head.

I wanted to know if prayer really worked. I mean, if I prayed for my parents to get back together, would God somehow answer that prayer? Or would I be putting my heart out there to God, wasting my time, praying in vain? I didn't want to get my hopes up that God would work a miracle if it wasn't going to happen. I decided to try a little experiment.

Rather than watering the flowers, I stepped out in faith, asking God to water them for me. As soon as I woke up the next morning, I raced outside. The ground was wet and the flowers looked vibrant; yes, it had rained.

Okay, so maybe it was a coincidence that it rained that night. But I remember it being a hot, cloudless day so perhaps God really did answer my prayer. But either way I continued to hope and pray that somehow God would bring my parents back together again.

The summer before my sophomore year in high school, my parents signed the divorce papers. And truthfully, between you and me, even after that I still held onto the hope that my parents would get back together, that is until my mom remarried seven years later.

God didn't intend for my parents to get a divorce, but why did he let it happen? He could have stopped it and brought them some sort of reconciliation. We all watch movies with Hollywood endings and may sometimes hear stories about God answering prayer, but what about all the times when God seems to remain silent, not keeping his promises to answer our prayers?

> "All things are possible with God,"

> Mark 10:27 (NIV)

Jesus said,

> "You may ask me for anything in my name, and I will do it."

> John 14:13 (NIV)

Yet, amid all the pain, it may seem like God is utterly absent.

Hope

There I was, sitting on the back-porch steps with Carolyn, thinking about the hope within me that kept me going.

"Have you ever listened to the song 'Bring It On' by Steven Curtis Chapman?" I remember asking her as we looked up at the stars together.

"No," she shook her head slowly.

"Well, it goes, 'Let the lightning flash, let the thunder roll, let the storms winds blow. Bring it on. Let me be made weak so I'll know of the strength of the One who's strong. Bring it on.'" I looked over at my sister. It hurt me to see her hurting so badly.

I took a deep breath. Divorce hurts. There's no denying that stark reality. It's as if a part of you, if not your entire family, belief system, and self-image, is killed, destroyed totally. Yet, even during the pain, there is always hope. Always.

I remember carefully choosing my words. As gently as I could, I explained to her the only thing that allowed me to get through the divorce was to believe that somehow God would turn it all for good.

> "And we know that in all things God works for the good of those who love him, who have been called according to his purpose."

> Romans 8:28 (NIV)

God didn't create or even necessarily intend for the bad things to take place, but he is faithful to take the bad and make good out of it. Romans 8 talks about the hope we have in Christ Jesus who frees us from all suffering. God has overcome all things, and we too are more than conquerors. And nothing -- not death, nor life nor divorce -- nothing can separate us from the love of God. Therefore, if God is for us, who can be against us?

Yes, crap happens. That's life. But God is good, and he is faithful to bring good out of even the worst situations. That's where our hope should focus. Somehow, someway God will turn all this for good. Therefore, I can say, amid all my pain and questions, "Bring it on!"

This isn't just some nice, fluffy Christian jargon. I genuinely believed every word. I needed to. This couldn't simply be a little cheer-up cliché; it had to be real. Even though I had no idea what exactly it meant, it was that innocent hope that literally kept me alive.

The Road Less Traveled

I had a decision to make. Was I going to get caught up in the coping mechanisms the world had to offer: drinking, drugs, smoking, partying? Or was I going to press into this God who promises to be with me no matter what, personally working in every situation I encountered? I was at a fork in the road.

With the encouragement of my friends at church, I chose the road less traveled. I chose to press into God and trust him. It was my hope in God's promise to turn all things for good that got me through all the brokenness.

In junior high, my youth pastor would challenge us to dream big and pursue God, digging deep in our

relationships with him. One day, after the divorce had
been announced, I asked my mom if I could talk with
Pastor Jamie one-on-one. We set up an appointment and I
went. In his office, he had a few big beanbag chairs that
we relaxed in as I shared what all was going on in my life.
He was super understanding and simply inspired me to
keep trusting God.

It was about that time in my life when a verse in
Romans became my favorite. I memorized it:

> "Be joyful in hope, patient in affliction, and
> faithful in prayer."

> Romans 12:12 (NIV)

The joy that I had wasn't from the divorce not
affecting me, but rather it was supernaturally generated
from the hope within me. This hope helped me to
persevere and patiently wait on God's faithfulness, while
trying to be consistent in prayer. Truthfully, I wasn't
always very good at prayer.

Now, what I didn't tell you before is that even though I
may have still prayed occasionally, over time the context
of my prayer changed. My original prayer was, "God, I
pray that my parents won't get a divorce." As things got
worse, I found myself praying, "But if my parents get
divorced, I pray that at least someone will be saved
through it."

In a way, I kind of made a deal with God. If my parents
weren't going to get back together, then I prayed he
would somehow turn this devastating situation around

and use it to save someone. I guess it's possible that if I hadn't changed my prayer and had kept asking God to heal my parents' marriage, things could have turned out a lot differently. But they didn't. And I certainly won't blame myself.

I want to pause here for a second and speak to all the kids out there: It's NOT your fault. Period. And parents: Don't EVER blame your kids. Okay? If you need someone to blame, blame Satan. He's the one who comes to steal, kill, and destroy. The battles we face are not against our own flesh and blood, it's against all that evil out there.

So, anyway, where was I? Hope.

> "Hold unswervingly to the hope you
> profess for he who promised is faithful."

Hebrews 10:23 (NIV)

Never let go of your hope in God's faithfulness to turn all things for good.

Faith in the Faithful

Music pounded deep into my very being. My heart beat with an overwhelming intensity inside my chest as I began to realize what had happened. Humbly I sat with tears flooding my eyes. I was surrounded by hundreds of high school students worshiping God on a cold winter night at a youth retreat in Wisconsin. It was my junior year in college, and I was a small group leader for sophomore and junior high school girls.

My amazing co-leader Morgan sat down next to me

and gave me a big hug. I felt a rush of joy and couldn't help but laugh. It was in this moment that I had realized God had answered my prayer from seven or eight years earlier. He had taken me through a journey that led me to this small group where I had the privilege of having two girls join and within a year declare Jesus as their Lord and Savior.

I can remember both those moments so clearly. It was incredible seeing the light bulb go on and the freedom that comes with making such a life-altering decision. As each girl prayed, desperately needing God's faithful intervention in her own life, I couldn't help but realize that I really didn't do anything; it was all God.

After years and years of hoping that God would be faithful to use the divorce for something good, it dawned on me that he had been faithful. He has carried me through the brokenness, and even though I'm still not fully healed and whole, he has been faithful to work intimately with me through it all. It was God who brought me through the divorce to a place where I could share my story of brokenness and healing with others, encouraging them to put their hope in God's faithfulness to somehow turn all things for good within their own lives.

You see, my hope wasn't so much in my parents getting back together as it was in God's goodness and faithfulness. Looking back, God has been incredibly good. He has been faithful. And he will continue to be good and faithful, not only to me, but also to you. God *will* be faithful.

I looked over at my sister. She stood up and walked

back inside. Silently I sat on the porch, thinking through our conversation. It was hard for me to talk to my own sister about the divorce, and it was even harder to face the judgment I expected to encounter from society.

Questions to Explore

- As I remember, my sister asked me, "How is the divorce affecting you?" How would you respond to this question?
- Have you ever felt like your parents' divorce was your fault? If so, what made you feel that way?
- What keeps you going? Is there anything specific that gives you hope?

4 STRIKEOUT

The last box was packed.

"Come on, Carmen!" I called as I stuffed the box in the tiny space left in the backseat of my mom's car. My beautiful beagle bounded down the back-porch steps toward me. Suddenly, she veered to the right, apparently intrigued by a new scent.

My mom started the car. I whistled. Carmen's head perked up, and she ran over to me, ears flopping with each step. I scooped her up in my arms, holding her close to my heart. I looked back at the white house with blue shutters. I didn't want to leave; I wanted to cry.

I hated every minute we were driving in the car because every minute took me farther away from my cherished home and closer to my mom's new apartment. When I was little I had a list of things I never wanted to do, ever:

1. Be a missionary,
2. Be a pastor, and
3. Live in an apartment.

Looking at the list now makes me laugh because I've basically done all three in some capacity. But as a freshman in high school, I was upset. I loathed the situation. I hated that I had to move out of my childhood home into an apartment with my mom. Living with my mom was fine, but living in an apartment was embarrassing.

That's how I felt. It was a huge cut to my pride. I wanted to live in a nice house with a big backyard, not a little apartment. This was one of the most humbling experiences I've had. Now I realize that where I live doesn't determine who I am, even despite my perceived stereotypes.

We arrived at the apartment and unloaded. My new bedroom was full of boxes and white walls. It was sad. I was sad. Sad. That's an understatement! I was shaken, upset, crushed. I was miserable. But I wanted to be strong for my parents, for my mom. I didn't want her to see and know how much I hated moving. I knew she was struggling with the whole thing so why would I be a burden to her?

So I hid the tears. I put on a poker face and left, murmuring under my breath to her that I was taking Carmen for a walk. The surroundings were unfamiliar to me, but it didn't matter. I just kept walking. Tears streamed down my face. I looked away whenever a car passed, ashamed that I was crying.

We walked and walked. To the same extent my parent's marriage brought happiness to our family, the divorce brought a deep sense of sadness.

When we got back from our walk, my mom was in her bedroom talking on the phone so I retreated to my own bedroom. I was exhausted. I collapsed on my bed and didn't want to move.

Lying in Bed

I was lying in bed, feeling completely alone. The boxes were gone, my room was organized, and I had so many posters on one wall that it looked like it was covered in wallpaper. I gently tossed my basketball up in the air and caught it as it came back down.

I gripped the basketball and couldn't help but think about my broken family. Slowly I loosened my grip and let the ball fall to the floor. The sudden noise startled my dog. Her collar jingled as she came over to the side of my bed. I reached down to pet her. I exhaled and closed my eyes.

My mind raced with questions. Why are my parents getting a divorce? Why my parents? Why do I have to live at this apartment? Will they have to sell the house?

A tear escaped and ran down my cheek. I sniffed. I wished I didn't have to live here. I wished everything was back to normal, that everything was okay.

I stopped petting Carmen, grabbed my pillow, and hugged it tightly to my chest. In that moment, I desperately needed someone, anyone, to hold me and reassure me that everything was going to be okay. I needed someone to sit with me while I cried. I needed someone to care.

I opened my eyes, looking up at the ceiling. My gaze followed my posters down to where my phone was sitting across the room from me. I stared at the phone.

Yes, I had friends and family members who cared about me. But it didn't feel like it at the time. Why didn't they ask me how I'm doing? Why didn't they call?

I just needed some encouragement, but instead I felt utterly alone. Was I depressed? I don't think so, even though my dad said I was. He was concerned that I might be clinically depressed, which made me think that maybe I was, even though I wasn't.

Yes, I was sad, even devastated. And I had full right to be! My parents were in the middle of a long, nasty divorce. Feeling upset, angry, sad, or numb is totally normal; it's okay. But it's not okay to wallow in it alone.

I was looking at the phone, wishing someone would call, feeling completely forgotten and alone. Yet why wouldn't I just pick up the phone and call someone? I didn't want to be a burden. It was getting late, and I didn't want to disturb anyone or rudely wake someone up.

I was stuck lying on my bed, wishing I wasn't alone and wishing for things to be better, but I didn't have the energy to do anything about it. Suddenly, Carmen jumped onto my bed and snuggled up next to me. Well, at least I had my dog.

The Bench

I played basketball and softball in high school. Truthfully, I wasn't very good at basketball. Most of the time during the game, if not the whole game, I would sit on the bench. The only point I scored during my high school career, I'm sure, was a single free-throw. Softball, however, was a different story. I was dubbed, "The Run Maker."

Okay, okay, so it was my mom who nicknamed me, "The Run Maker," but I was still rather fast and could steal my way around the bases successfully.

During one game, I was positioned on third base, hoping either my teammate would hit me home or the catcher would drop the ball, giving me an opportunity to steal. The pitcher took her stance, watching the catcher's hand signals. She nodded. I leaned back so that I could get more momentum.

The pitch! I sprinted off the base to get a good leadoff.

Strike! I immediately pivoted and ran back to third base. Suddenly, the softball hit my shoulder at about 60 mph. The catcher had tried to throw it back to the third basemen to tag me for the out, but slipped and the ball caught my shoulder. Pain shot down my arm as I fell into the dirt.

I slid and grabbed third base before they could recover the ball to tag me out. My coach helped me up and asked if I was okay. Slowly I rotated my arm and winced in pain. I told him I was okay, but he called for a replacement runner from the bench. Reluctantly, I jogged off the field.

A teammate tossed me my glove to see if I could throw. It was my right shoulder, my throwing arm, that was hit. I tried to throw the ball to her, but the pain was too great. Grabbing a bat, I started swinging to test it out, but there was no way. I was out of the game. I was furious. That catcher took me out of the game.

I was upset, but sitting out for the rest of the game made sense. When playing sports, if you get physically hurt you walk it off unless it's more serious. If the injury is more serious, then the coach benches you because you clearly wouldn't play as well. You could easily hurt yourself even worse, possibly taking you out of the entire season rather than just one game.

But when it comes to being hurt emotionally, why is it so difficult to acknowledge the pain? It's important to acknowledge the pain, let others encourage you, and trust the Holy Spirit to do the difficult heart work.

It took me out of the game. Sure, we don't want to be on the bench for the entire game every game, but it's okay to sit it out for a little while. It's okay to let others go to bat for you. It's okay to pick up the phone and make that call.

And as we acknowledge the pain and let others encourage us, God will be faithful to bring healing. We can trust him to take care of our families and us.

Dare You to Move

I remember the moment I contemplated suicide. I was in the living room at my mom's apartment, heading to my bedroom. The hallway to the front door was on my left.

My mom's big wooden computer desk was to my right.

Sometimes we get so desperate and feel utterly stuck in this pain that we need a way to escape. Some people drown their pain with alcohol. Others numb it with drugs. Some expose their internal pain through external pain by cutting.

For me, I didn't want to drink or do drugs because I hated the idea of losing any sort of control over my body. I didn't want to smoke because inhaling nastiness didn't sound like fun. I didn't like the idea of cutting because I was already hurting enough as it was. Why would I want to inflict more pain upon myself?

So instead, my reaction was to lie in bed and stare at the phone. But then a song came to mind. During the warm-up for one of my basketball games earlier that week, they played a song by the band Switchfoot:

> "I dare you to move.
> I dare you to lift yourself up off the floor.
> I dare you to move."

That song played repeatedly in my mind as I laid in bed. I had a choice to make. I picked up the basketball that was on the ground next to my bed. Was my life worth living? The song kept playing in my head.

> "Maybe redemption has stories to tell…
> Where can you run to escape from yourself?
> Where you gonna go? Where you gonna go?
> Salvation is here."

Thoughts of suicide had flooded my head. In that moment, I made one of the most important decisions of my life. I decided suicide was not an option. Drinking, drugs, cutting, suicide, none of those were options for dealing with the pain. I wasn't going to do it.

I tossed the basketball into the air and caught it as it came back down. Yes, I was going to lie in bed and cry, but I would also get back up. I was not going to stay down.

Slowly I sat up in bed. Reaching out, I gently pet my dog, who was still next to me. I stood up and looked out the window.

Sometimes the sky is cloudy; sometimes it's sunny. But no matter what, no matter how dark the night is, morning always comes. Even amid the pain and sadness, we can trust God with our hearts, and we can dare to persevere.

Life goes on. There's redemption. There's hope.

Comfort Blanket

From right field, I could easily see the home sideline full of lawn chairs. The moms and dads of the girls on our team would huddle together and bundle up on chilly game days. They would chit chat, laugh, and applaud all good play. A lot of the time my mom was sitting there with them, bragging about her baby girl.

Having my mom at my softball games was very important to me. I knew she was proud of me and it gave me reason to play better, providing entertainment for my adoring fan. One time there was a fly ball hit into the outfield. No one was on base and I could tell it would be a simple catch. So instead of sprinting to get under the ball for the easy catch, I jogged toward the ball and at the last second, made a dramatic dive to catch it. The runner was out, ending the inning. The crowd cheered.

My mom's presence made a huge difference. Having people on the sidelines cheering us on gives us the endurance and inspiration to persevere, to get up from the floor or out of bed. Even my dog Carmen, a constant companion as I switched back and forth every week between living at my mom's and dad's, was a source of comfort.

As we persevere through our pain and sadness, God will comfort us and renew our hope.

I was under great pressure, far beyond my ability to endure, so that I despaired of life itself. But this wasn't so I would rely on myself, but on God, the God of comfort who comforts us in our troubles. We can then in turn to comfort others in trouble with the same comfort we ourselves have received from God.

It's okay to be sad; it's good to feel the pain and cry. It hurts. That's the reality. And that's okay. As we acknowledge our pain, we can run to God for comfort. He will comfort us and fill us with hope. The Holy Spirit is even called our "Comforter."

> "...We know that suffering produces perseverance; perseverance, character; and character, hope. And hope does not put us to shame, because God's love has been

poured out into our hearts through the Holy Spirit, who has been given to us."

Romans 5:3-5 (NIV)

One time, I was so broken that I retreated to my room, sat on the bed in the fetal position and trembled as I cried. I felt completely betrayed, stabbed in the back. My heart hurt.

I cried out to God for comfort and he heard me. Suddenly I felt like I was wrapped up in a big comfy blanket. His comfort bombarded me immediately and truthfully, I was totally thrown off. I couldn't help but laugh.

God will comfort us and as we continue to persevere, our hope will be renewed.

Questions to Explore

- What feelings emerge when you think about the divorce? Anger? Sadness? Confusion? Embarrassment?
- Name some things that you do to cope with these emotions. Are these healthy responses or are there some better approaches that you can take?
- I dare you to move; I dare you to trust Jesus. Take a moment to talk with God about what's going on in your life, and ask him to walk with you through this journey.

5 HELLO?

"You didn't know?" My dad put down the remote and looked at me from across the living room.

I leaned against the stair railing to steady myself. A light-hearted conversation about what show my dad was watching on TV had weaved its way into a disheartening update. He reached for the bag of microwave popcorn. I slowly shook my head.

"Nope. I didn't." I tried hard not to let my voice crack. "When did that happen?"

"A month ago."

"Oh. Okay." I didn't care to inquire for more details, so I grabbed my textbooks and headed up the stairs to my bedroom.

I had just begun my sophomore year in high school, and now the divorce papers were finally signed. Years after the announcement, it was now official.

Everything felt so surreal. It was done. The hopes I

had of my parents working things out were pretty much crushed.

I didn't want people to know. The truth is, I was embarrassed of my family, or lack thereof. Yes, I was embarrassed.

Most people get embarrassed when they trip up the stairs, put their shirt on backwards, or say something stupid. I was embarrassed because my parents got divorced, and I didn't know how other people would respond. Would they look down on me? Would they think poorly of my parents? I mean, my parents are great people and don't deserve that.

I felt like I had a dark shadow following me, and I wanted to hide it. I didn't want to be judged; I didn't want to be labeled.

Sometimes it feels like people around us, or even ourselves, keep sticking all these, "Hello, my name is ..." labels all over us. And the blanks are filled with negative things that make us feel rejected. These are things we don't want people to see, especially if we believe them ourselves.

Labels like, "Hello, my name is failure." Or I'm "worthless" and "boring." It's like your forehead is marked with "loser" or "victim" is written on your arm. Maybe there's a label on your back that reads "stupid." Just kick me now.

Labels cover us. You feel "ashamed" and "hopeless," "confused" and "helpless." The label on your heart says, "I'm abandoned" or "I'm rejected." Hello, my name is "judged."

Why? Perhaps it's because we live in a broken world full of broken people who desperately want not to be broken. So rather than finding healing, they ignore the problem. They push the blame onto others. They move the spotlight from themselves onto the person next to them so that they don't feel so broken.

Or perhaps I should say "we" rather than "they."

When focusing on the speck of dust in your eye, the plank in mine suddenly doesn't look so big. If others focus on how horrible your labels are, their labels don't seem as bad. Consequently, we end up with negative labels all over us, but these labels aren't true.

Fear of Rejection

My high school classes were going just fine. For the first time ever, I was kind of enjoying my history class, but English was just as lame as ever. My favorite class had always been math, but this year I had a teacher who would spit while he talked; needless to say, I sat in the back. Chemistry was the best, and at one point, I accidentally lit a big walnut on fire. Oops.

There was nothing too out of the ordinary. School was okay. Homework was piling up and projects were underway. After riding the bus from school back to my mom's apartment and taking Carmen for a walk, I sat down on a stool at the counter that separated the kitchen from the living room. I grabbed the wireless phone from its cradle around the corner.

The new school phone directory had just come out. I reached for it and looked at the cover. There was a drawing of an elaborate castle positioned high on a hill. My high school literally looked like a castle on top of a hill overlooking a lake. It was pretty cool. We were the "Hilltoppers." We didn't really have a mascot. What we had was a guy dressed in a wrestling uniform, wearing a cape and running around holding a stick with a castle on it. Like I said, we were so cool.

I slowly flipped through the phone directory, looking for a friend I was doing a project with. L... M... N... I stopped.

Hmm...

This would be the first year I would have a different address. Weird. I turned the page.

O... P...

I placed my index finger at the top of the page and slowly scanned down until I stopped at my name. My heart suddenly sank.

"No. This is not happening," I said under my breath. I was angry; I was disappointed.

You see, the phone directory would first list the student's name and phone number followed by their parents' names and then address. This year's edition of the school phone directory not only had a different address, but only my mom was listed. It was like I was fatherless. It made sense that only my mom would be listed since it was her address, but the reality was disheartening.

Once again I felt ashamed. Now everyone was going to know. It was public knowledge. I no longer lived with both my mom and dad. They were separated; they were divorced. It was embarrassing, and I was afraid of people finding out.

Rather than announcing it to the whole world, I just wanted to hide in a corner. Why did they have to print the phone directory like that? What if they judge me? What if they look down on my family or think poorly of my parents? What if they see me as ...?

There were those labels popping up again. It was like I was being covered in them all over again. I didn't want people seeing me like that. I didn't want to be labeled.

Identity

I didn't want to be labeled because I was more than the divorce. Who I am is not defined by an event, family problems, or past mistakes. Rather, my identity lies in who God made me to be. It's like what the pastor spoke about in youth group recently. God is good and created everything good, and that included me. I was made in the image of God.

Hmm...

I glanced over at my mom's Bible sitting on the counter. It was in a burgundy leather case. Grabbing it, I unzipped the case and opened the book. It opened at Exodus 3 where Moses was leading his flock across the wilderness. He ended up on a mountain called Horeb and saw a bush on fire. It turns out that God was just doing his thing and showing up in a fun, crazy way. God called Moses over to have what became an incredible, life-changing conversation. As God revealed the mind-blowing adventure to which he was calling Moses, God also revealed his identity to Moses by proclaiming his name: Yahweh.

Before, God had remained nameless because his holiness is so great and his people held him in such high respect that no one could speak his name. In fact, even the Hebrew word Yahweh is truly unpronounceable. It was never spoken, but only written. Yahweh is translated in the English Bible as the LORD. It means, "I am who I am."

I continued to scan the footnotes. God could have given himself any name, but he chose the name "I Am," reflecting that his identity was not based on events, circumstances, or even relationships, but on his being. Since we are made in God's image, our identity is not wrapped up in what we do, our environment, or even our past, but simply in who we are, who God created us to be.

After God proclaimed his name, he went on to describe what that name meant. He is merciful, compassionate, gracious, slow to anger, rich in love and faithfulness, unfailing, and forgiving. We were created for the same.

You are loved, forgiven, and an important part of the family of God. Whether you believe in God or not, you are his cherished kid. You are chosen and accepted, and given great purpose. You were intricately created with the perfect combination of passions, talents, and abilities that makes you unique. There is no one like you.

And God has given you a name. Your name is not the negative labels that people around you, or even society, stick on you. No, your identity is not defined by the event of divorce, but by God's never ending love and grace. No longer should we wear the label that says, "Hello, my name is judged." Rather, write in "loved."

Breaking Out of the Box

I slid off the stool and walked into the kitchen. Grabbing a glass from the cabinet, I poured some water and took a nice long drink. The phone directory still sat on the counter with the phone right next to it. I looked back at it and let my mind continue to wander.

By accepting God's love and grace, we are given a clean slate, and there is no longer any reason to fear judgment or rejection.

Right?

But why?

We can have full confidence because God is love, so his perfect love drives out fear since fear has to do with punishment, but since we live in him and he in us, we do not stand condemned. Though people may judge and condemn us out of fear, Jesus did not come to condemn. So as we are in relationship with him through faith, we are given life and are freed from condemnation because of his grace.

"Yeah, I guess that makes sense," I heard myself think out loud.

I took another drink of water and returned to the stool. My mom's Bible still lay open in front of me. I set the glass down and closed it.

Why should I fear my high school's phone directory? Why should I let my life be manipulated by the judgments of the world around me? Where's the freedom in that?

It was like I was letting the world box me in. Picture it. I am encased in a thick glass box. And in this glass box, I am stuck with the shadow of divorce stalking me. I try to find a way out, but there is no exit, or at least that's how it seemed.

Sometimes our view of the world is off. We tend to care more about what others think than what God thinks. Their opinions of us, though many times false, seem more important than God's truth about us. We fear man rather than being secure in God's love. We see others as big and God as small.

Yet God is big and others are small. God knows us inside and out. His word is true and so much more powerful than the lies the world feeds us about ourselves.

I want to escape this glass box. I desperately want to break free and soar. So I keep hitting the glass ceiling in an attempt to escape. How can I break free?

Take off the negative labels. It's not easy, but you can do it. You can push past. You don't have to be boxed in by what others think. All those labels society puts on you, rip them off your shirt, and throw them in the garbage. They don't belong on you.

The glass will finally break. Gritting my teeth, yes, I will struggle to pull myself through the jagged hole in the ceiling. But, with all my strength, I will push myself past the brokenness, out of the box. I will be free to soar.

Label Free

We've all probably had dreams about flying, soaring high into the air with no worries, leaving everything behind. Slicing through the white, fluffy clouds and feeling the warm sun on our faces, like Peter Pan.

Being free from society's negative stereotypes makes you feel like you can fly and instead of your shadow being those labels, your shadow is the grace of God, faithfully staying with you no matter what. By his grace, we can break free from the box society puts us in and strip off the negative labels, replacing them with truth.

The old labels are gone. Instead we now have labels like, "Hello, my name is forgiven." Or labels like, "I'm accepted" and "worthy of love". You feel "respectable" and "hopeful" and "strong." The new label on your heart says, "I'm cherished" or "I'm important." These are labels of truth.

I shook my head and snapped back into reality. Slowly I hit the keys on the phone and brought it up to my ear. As I heard the familiar sound of ringing, I closed the phone book, gave it one last look, and tossed it to the other side of the counter.

In high school, when I was flipping through the phone book, I wanted to tear it to shreds or be a pyro and light it on fire. But now, I'm not afraid anymore. I am who God says I am, not as other people label me. God's love and grace brought me freedom, and the faithfulness of God that I have experienced empowers me to encourage others to hold onto this same hope.

Honestly, I'm being vulnerable with you as I share my story. I'm opening my heart to you and writing about not only of God's faithfulness, but also my deepest pains and struggles in life.

Not a lot of people are willing to do that. But I believe you're worth it. You're worth me being vulnerable and sticking my neck out there for you. You're worth me taking the time to be the voice amid the lies to tell you the truth.

And the truth is, you are so much more than any negative label that people put on you. As you believe this and believe the truth about who you really are, you too can speak truth into others people's lives.

Questions to Explore

- Beyond just the physical characteristics, who do you see when you look at yourself in the mirror?
- What type of names have people (peers, teachers, family, etc.) labeled you with over the years?
- Which truth or positive label that I mentioned in this chapter most resonates with you? Why?

6 LETTING GO

This was it. The winter youth retreat everyone at church raved about. Hundreds of high school students flooded into a large warehouse room with a big stage up front and rows upon rows of uncomfortable metal chairs set up on the cold cement floor. My friends and I shed our coats and sat down on the right side, halfway back.

We talked about the team competitions as we waited for the worship band to get on stage. We had just come from team competitions outside where we played an intense game of tug-o-war in the snow. We were totally winning until suddenly the rope broke.

The worship band started to play and we stood, singing our hearts out. Then came the guest speaker. I leaned forward in my chair as he challenged us not to let others live our faith for us, but to give God everything. That's what Jesus wants, not just what we are confident about, but he wants all of us.

The speaker encouraged us to pray, "God, take me, bless me, break me." No matter where we are in life, or what we're going through, whether that's trouble at school, or problems with friends, a death in the family, or if your parents are going through a divorce, we should surrender it all to God.

As soon as the speaker said the word "divorce," it was like someone stabbed me in the gut, like ripping off a nasty old bandage that had been covering up a wound that never healed properly. I was surprised at the deep hurt and shame I felt. He said the word "divorce" a second time, and pain coursed through my heart again.

The speaker finished and the worship band began playing again. Quickly I retreated to the back of the room and sat with my face buried in my hands, letting the tears run down my cheeks and drip to the floor. I sniffed, wiped my eyes, and reached for my journal. I brushed my hand over the green cover and flipped it open. With my pencil, I wrote:

> Every time he talked about divorce I was
> on the verge of crying (like I am right now
> as I write about it). What does this mean?
> Am I not over my parents' divorce?

I was now a senior in high school. It had been more than two years since my parents had signed the papers and more than four since they told us they were getting a divorce. Time brings healing, right? So why am I still crying over this?

Even though time goes by and it seems like we should

be healed from the divorce already, we may not be over it yet.

Not Over It

There I was, clenching my journal in one hand and my pencil in the other. I was surprised at how broken I felt. An hour earlier, I was totally fine, or so I thought. But as soon as the speaker talked about divorce, all the walls I had built up to protect my heart from experiencing the pain of the divorce came crashing down. I was faced with the reality that I hadn't yet come to terms with it.

But why hadn't I learned to accept it? I continued to write with tears streaming down my face:

> Am I not over my parents' divorce? Did I not cry enough when they split, and it's just been bottled up in me?

I paused to think. I shook my head slowly and took a deep breath.

> I don't know what it could be. Is it that my parents are moving on, but I'm not willing to do so? Is that it?

One day I was spending time with my mom and sister. During the conversation, my sister asked my mom about her boyfriend. Boyfriend? What? I had no idea my mom had a boyfriend. It turned out she had signed up for an online dating service and had been talking to a gentleman who lived several hours north of us.

As for my dad, he didn't really have a girlfriend, but he would hang out with female friends. And at nearly every dinner, he would joke around about dating women. Ugh. I absolutely hated when he talked about it. He thought he was funny; I wanted to punch him.

This is one of the hardest things kids of divorce must go through: having their parents date other people. I don't think parents realize how much their personal lives affect the kids.

My mom remarried six years after the divorce was finalized. By that point in my life, I had healed a lot from the divorce, yet it was still very hard to see her kiss a man other than my father on her wedding day. I feel like most parents would assume that by six years' post-divorce, the kid would be over it and not have any issue with the parent getting remarried. For me, not so much.

Today, as a youth worker, I have seen many teenagers struggle with their parents' divorces and in addition, must put up with their parents' poor choices in their own internal healing processes and dating relationships. Whether that's a dad dating a woman before he's technically divorced, and therefore still married, or a mom who moves in with her boyfriend after the divorce and expects the kids to be totally okay with living with some strange man. Okay? No. Not okay.

Thankfully neither of my parents were morally unethical nor super insensitive to my feelings or needs. Yet, as a teenager, seeing my parents move on was still difficult. And me trying to move on was even harder.

How would my family be restored if my parents never

got back together? How would my parents ever get back together if they were seeing other people? I had been holding on so tightly to the idea of my family, that I wasn't letting myself process the pain and heal.

Holding onto Sand

"Why can't I move on?" I gripped the pencil tighter as I continued to write. My chin quivered and shivers went up and down my spine as I realized the answer.

Because it is my family.

I went back and underlined "my." For a moment, I just sat there staring at the words I had written in my journal. This wasn't just anyone's family; this was *my* family. It was like I was entitled to a perfect, whole family. I felt like I owned it and should have had full control over it. Yet we really don't have control over the world around us.

We tend to worry about grades, work deadlines, friends, cars, health, sports, etc. And I think we worry so much because we want things to go a certain way. We get caught up in games of power struggle and manipulation. But no matter how hard we try, we aren't in control and can't always make things go the way we want them to go. Over and over God tells us not to worry, but to trust him. He is the one in control. He holds all things in his hands.

I could hear the gentle, soft voice of God deep within my spirit. It wasn't in an audible voice that God spoke, but it was still clear. God began to give me an analogy to help me understand. I looked down at my hand.

Imagine your hand is cupped and full of sand, a huge heap of sand. Some of the sand slips through the cracks between your fingers. In response, you close your fingers around the pile of sand, trying to hold on, not wanting to let it go. But the more you try so desperately to hold on, the more you apply pressure, the more the sand will slip out of your hand.

You see, the sand represented my family. The divorce caused the sand to slip through my fingers. As I tried to cling onto the idea of my perfect family, not wanting to let it go or change my view of the situation, the more I saw my family crumbling before me. I still held to this ideal of a perfect family and was stubborn to change, stubborn to the reality of the divorce. Because of not accepting the truth about my family, I wasn't allowing myself to heal from the brokenness.

I had been holding on and holding on to something I could no longer control. The more we try to hold on and control things, the more things tend to go out of control.

Open Handed

The sand analogy doesn't stop there. Yes, if you have a pile of sand in your hand and you close your fingers around it trying to hold onto it, the sand will slip through. But if you open your hand, the sand won't fall.

It sounds backwards, but the lack of pressure allows for the sand not to move. The next time you're at a beach, try it. Maybe a couple grains will get through, but for the most part, the sand will stay in your hand.

"It's time to open your hand and trust me," I felt God say to me.

Trust. What is trust? When you close your eyes, lock your knees, and free fall backwards, hoping the person standing behind you will catch you before you hit the ground? Trust isn't something to be taken lightly.

What if I truly trusted God to be in control of my life instead of me? That's kind of a big deal. I think a lot of people down play it, making it out not to be a big deal, maybe in hope that people will "trust" God without questioning just so people feel good about it. But trusting God isn't just some sweet little feel-good thing we pretend to do.

Trusting God means full dependence on him. It means giving up control of what's going on around you and truly believing that he has a good plan and he's walking with you. It doesn't mean life will suddenly become super easy, but it does mean you'll never be alone because God is right there with you, holding you in his hands, never letting go.

But *why* would I trust him? Well, why would I trust anyone, for that matter? Because those who love me, know me. I know they will do things in my best interests and would never purposefully hurt me.

God knows you inside and out; he knows you far better than anyone else, even yourself. He created you. He knows what makes you happy and what makes you sad. He knows the hard things with which you're struggling. He knows.

God knew I was completely broken and I missed my

family. He knew I missed all the fun memories, like the time I procrastinated on creating a diorama for school. The night before it was due, my entire family gathered around the dining room table and helped me build an elaborate one out of random things we found around the house. God was there. He understood that I miss those times. And sometimes I still miss doing stuff like that with my family. God knows.

And he's been there too. Jesus went through pretty much everything we can go through and more. He understands. He sympathizes with us. He gets it. He likes you. He loves you. He genuinely cares about you. He wants us to walk through life with him, and let him be in control, working everything out for the good as we trust him.

It was time for me to let go of the idealized utopia of a family that I wished would come true, and trust that God would be faithful to redeem what was left of my family. Rather than being the one trying to control things in vain, I needed to let God hold me in his hands and be in control.

Goodbye

I had been hiding from the reality of the divorce. I wasn't letting go of my perfect family. It was falling through my fingers, and I had no control over it slipping away.

All throughout junior and senior high school I was never really at a point where I could truly acknowledge my pain and begin the healing process. I never actually realized I needed to go through an intentional healing process. I just thought I would eventually "get over it." But obviously, that wasn't how it worked.

I closed my journal and let the worship music flood my mind: "My heart and my soul, I give you control. Consume me from the inside out, Lord."

I needed to be vulnerable enough with a God who knew and loved me to let him in. I needed to trust him with the divorce, my family, and my own brokenness. He was beckoning me to allow him to walk me through the painful memories, facing my greatest fears and battling all the mind games. He would lead me through this healing process, working through the pain and rebuilding relationships. And together we would discover the answer to the hard questions like, "What is home?"

I set my journal and pencil down on the empty seat next to me. Looking across the room, I saw a box of tissues. Slowly I stood up, walked over, and grabbed one. I blew my nose and sat back down. I just sat there for a few minutes, soaking in the new revelation. I took a long, deep breath.

I held out my clenched fist in front of me.

"Okay, God." I whispered under my breath. Slowly I opened my hand, my palm facing up. "Here, take it all. I'm letting go."

I felt a sense of peace fall over me.

Slowly I could feel my heart opening to God as I gave up control and trusted him to hold all things in his hands. I was now at a point where God could bring healing, redemption, and freedom. Finally, I could face my deepest fears.

Questions to Explore

- Have your parents dated or remarried? Was your reaction similar or different to my reaction?
- Are you still holding tightly onto your parents' marriage like I was, while watching the "sand" slip through your fingers?
- How do you feel about opening your hand and trusting Jesus?

7 FEAR

My heart was pounding as I ran down the street. I sucked in air, feeling my lungs burn. I looked behind me; something or someone was chasing me. A powerful sense of fear coursed through my body.

Immediately I jerked awake, lying in bed dumbfounded. It was the Monday before Easter my freshman year in college, and I had just experienced the first dream I've had since I was a little kid. What made this even more interesting was that only a month or so earlier a Christian I met at a friend's house was encouraging me and believed that God would start speaking to me through dreams.

The following night I had a continuation of that dream. Horrified, I was running, running, running away from something. Frantically my feet raced across the cold cement street toward a building. I flung open the door, trying to get away, looking for protection. The fear I was experiencing was so intense. As I entered the room, I suddenly saw Rob, and all my fear instantly went away.

I woke up from that dream, knowing what the fear was, what I was running away from, but I didn't understand what to do about it. I didn't know what God was trying to tell me through these two dreams.

You see, at that time, Rob was my best guy friend and I was in love with him, yet even though he had asked me to be his girlfriend, I had turned him down twice. I wanted God to tell me if it was okay to date him because I didn't want to get caught up in a relationship when that wasn't what God wanted. I mean, I was in college now. I had dated a couple guys in high school, but that was just high school. Now that I was in college, the idea of marriage was floating around in my mind, and I didn't want to date and marry someone who I would later regret.

What I didn't realize was that I wasn't simply being cautious; I was acting out of fear. I was afraid of ending up like my parents – divorced. I had been hurt so badly by the breakdown of my family that I didn't even want the love and joy that comes from a good, healthy family because I was terrified of being hurt all over again.

Consequently, I was running, running away from that fear rather than facing it. But how do I break free from this fear? Was I running to Rob when I should be going to God? Did God want to use my relationship with Rob to take the fear away? Or was God trying to tell me something totally different?

On Good Friday, I woke up and suddenly knew what the dream meant. God was going to use my relationship with Rob to take away my fear. Jesus can use a lot of different people to break us free from our fear, and not just a boyfriend or girlfriend. He can use friends and mentors and counselors. But the important thing isn't how Jesus breaks us free. The important thing is that he does, that we allow God's love to transform us. Though divorce provokes intense fear, his love breaks us free.

Failed Love

Rob and I officially started dating on Easter Sunday. I had been eagerly waiting for that day for months; I was like a little kid anticipating opening a huge Christmas present. I pictured myself joyfully skipping around my dorm telling all my friends the exciting news that we were now dating. Everything was going to be wonderful.

Yet when he asked and I finally answered yes, my reaction surprised me. The fear that I knew I had in theory suddenly became vividly real, and my stomach doubled over in knots. One of our friends noticed we were holding hands as we walked back to the dorms so Rob happily explained how we were now dating. I felt sick, but did everything I could to hide it with a weak smile.

Everything within me wanted to run away. I was thinking Arizona. I wanted to get out of there and just flee from the problem rather than face it. Some of us may feel like running away, while others may feel like totally shutting down, hiding under our blankets, and trying to ignore the problem. Or perhaps some people prefer fighting, attacking the problem or something, anything, to feel like maybe their efforts are making a difference, frantically wanting to manipulate change even when they can't.

Either way we are faced with a controlling fear of experiencing pain again. It was as if I was standing on the high dive, peering past my toes, over the edge, looking down, down, down at the water below and not having any clue how to swim. I'm supposed to just jump right in, do a backflip, and somehow not drown.

Some people are afraid of heights, public speaking, or spiders. I'm not easily scared by stuff like that, but what I do tend to be afraid of is the absence of love. I'm afraid of being abandoned or rejected.

I have been neglected and ignored by my best friends and even family members at different times throughout my life, leaving me with a disappointed heart full of scars. Trust was broken and never restored. We long to be loved, but when others try to love us, they fail. My parents tried to restore their marriage, but they couldn't. Love failed.

I try to love people, yet I mess up and end up hurting the very people I love most. And once we are hurt, we don't want to open up and risk being loved again in fear of not being loved. It's only natural to put up a wall to protect ourselves from experiencing that again. When love fails, it provokes intense fear of not being loved.

The Deep End

I'm not a great swimmer. Sure, I can doggy paddle, but if you stick me in the ocean or wave pool, you better go call a lifeguard. Unfortunately, I've had a few near drowning experiences. In fact, the summer after we started dating, I was at a waterpark in Michigan with Rob. We decided to head to the wave pool. I was very nervous because of my track record when it comes to swimming, but I was kind of enjoying bouncing up and down with the waves. That is until the big waves started coming and I was getting tired. I started taking in water and gasping for air. Reaching out, I grabbed Rob's shoulder. Thankfully he was lifeguard certified and immediately helped me back to the shallow end.

That's how I felt. I was caught in way over my head, drowning in the fear of being hurt again. I was gasping for air, trying to break free. I needed to be rescued. On a weekend retreat, God spoke clearly to me. It was early spring, and I was outside overlooking an empty pool in the distance.

You don't have to jump off the high dive right into the deep end, I felt God speak to me. Gently he reassured me and explained that I could slowly wade in, gradually working my way from the shallow area into the deep end. I could take my time to learn how to swim.

I completely believe that God can break people free from fear in an instant, but I also know it can be a journey of learning to trust God and be loved by him. Breaking free from fear is learning to trust Jesus, be loved by him, and understand that he knows you and will be faithful to take care of you.

"And so we know and rely on the love God

has for us. God is love. Whoever lives in love lives in God, and God in them. This is how love is made complete among us so that we will have confidence on the day of judgment: In this world we are like Jesus. There is no fear in love. But perfect love drives out fear, because fear has to do with punishment. The one who fears is not made perfect in love. We love because he first loved us."

1 John 4:16-19 (NIV)

We fear being rejected or abandoned because we don't feel like we deserve to be loved, that we aren't good enough. There is nothing we can offer that would make someone truly love us. There is nothing we could do to stop a loved one from hurting us. But when we understand that God is the ultimate source for love and his love is unconditional and isn't based on our performance, we can fearlessly bask in his love.

Even though I've been rejected and abandoned by different people throughout my life, God will never leave me. Sure, people will continue to fail me, but Jesus is always with me, and his love never fails.

I'm not talking about the cutesy "Jesus Loves You" cliché people like to throw around in a sad attempt of encouraging someone when they don't want to deal with the messy issues in a person's life. I'm talking about experiencing a radical, life-transforming encounter with the powerful love of God. This is the kind of love that stoops down into the mud, wraps you up in his arms, and lifts you out. This is love that truly cares and cherishes you. The kind of love that doesn't stop no matter what you do or who you think you are. This is love that loves even when you don't love back. The kind that never gives up even if everyone else, including you, have. This is love that knows you inside and out, and will be faithful to take care of you. This is love that never fails.

Feeling Numb

Would you rather experience great love, but at the expense of feeling great pain, or would you rather feel little pain, but at the expense of experiencing little love?

This fear of not being loved was so gripping that it stopped me from loving and allowing others to love me. I felt numb all over. I closed my heart so much that I could barely feel. As a little girl, I was sensitive and compassionate, but now my passion had waned, and I felt the light in my eyes dim. I longed to be loved and to have close relationships, but I wouldn't let myself.

It was so deep that subconsciously I would see the bad in a close friend or mentor and dislike them so that when conflict arose or time passed, the distance wouldn't hurt. My dad would tell me he loved me every time he dropped me off at my high school in the morning or ended a phone call with me. Every time I would say "you too" because it was easier than saying "I love you."

Those are the three hardest words for me to say and really mean because they are so powerful. Yet at the same time, those words don't seem to hold any significance if someone else directs them at me. In one ear and out the other. If someone hugged me I would feel it on the outside, but I wouldn't let their love sink in past my skin to my heart.

Rather than pressing into relationships, I pulled away. I got to the point when I stopped to look around and realized I had many friends, but they were all shallow. I no longer had any close ones. So I found new friends. We would have lots of fun and get to know each other, but once we got too close something would happen and the relationship would die. This was a cycle I needed to end.

I had to ask myself this question: Would I rather feel deeply or feel nothing? Yet, at the same time, you can't just feel nothing because one day the numbness will catch up to you and you'll feel the pain and loneliness that it caused.

Yes, opening myself up to be loved also opens me up to be hurt. But even though water can kill, it's essential to bringing life. It was time for me to confront these life-sucking fears. By facing our fears and trusting God's love, we can break free.

So here I go, stepping into the pool.

On the Floor

I needed to let myself feel and be open to the possibility of being hurt so that I could be loved. I decided to trust God and let God use Rob to break me free from these fears. I decided to let Rob in.

One night, I was so full of fear and pain that I was shaking. Rob and I were standing in my dorm lobby.

People occasionally walked by, but I didn't care. I dropped to my knees and laid down on the carpet. I buried my head in my arms.

Rob slowly lowered himself to the floor and began whispering truth into my ear. He told me he wasn't going to leave me, and he reminded me of God's never-ending love. Tears streamed down my face as the truth seeped deep into my heart. I finally allowed myself to cry.

Sometimes we just need to fall to the floor before God and cry. It's okay to be real with him and admit our fears. He won't condemn us; he'll give us life. He wants to hear our hearts. He doesn't just want the good we can offer; he wants the pain and struggles, the doubts and fears. He wants it all.

As we are humbly on the floor before Jesus, he will pick us back up again, dust us off, and walk with us. He's our protector and our provider. Yes, you will be hurt again. I've been hurt over and over, but God brings healing. And even though I want to close myself off again in fear, being loved by friends and family is worth the risk.

Jesus is our lifeguard, gradually and patiently wading in with us. He is right there when we start getting in over our heads. We can reach out and grab him. He will save us. And the more we swim, the better we get at it. The more I allow myself to love and be loved, the more I will experience the great love of God.

Slowly over time I was breaking free from my fear. As I opened my heart up, allowing others to love me, the numbness left and my passion was renewed. A spark within my soul ignited, and I felt so alive.

This newfound freedom burned within me, daring me to reach out and love others without the expectation of them loving me in return. I made the choice not to hold back from loving others in fear of being rejected or abandoned. It was refreshing. I was experiencing a piece of this unconditional love the Bible tells us about. Being free from these fears of not being loved, frees us up to love and be loved.

Finally, I was allowing myself to feel again, to feel love and pain. Now it was time to sift through the pain I had kept bottled up all these years.

Questions to Explore

- People react to conflict in three different ways: fight, flight, or freeze. Do you tend to feel like running away, freeze up in a situation, or fight back? How does this reaction affect you and those around you?
- Going deeper than spiders and heights, what frightens you? How has the divorce sparked fear in your heart?
- Let yourself feel for a moment. Talk to God and write down what's going on inside of your heart.

8 PAIN

My fingers gently rested on the old worn keys of the upright piano. Music filled the room, and I felt a sense of relief. I took a deep breath and began to sing, "Every blessing you pour out I'll turn back to praise. When the darkness closes in Lord, still I will say. Blessed be the name of the Lord, blessed be your name ..."

My voice cracked, and my body trembled. I pushed myself to continue. "Blessed be your name, when the sun's shining down on me, the world's all that it should be ..."

A tear trickled down my cheek. My heart burned with pain, and it took me every ounce of strength to finish the verse. "Blessed be your name on the road marked with suffering ..."

I stopped. My hands went limp, and I buried my head in my arms, sobbing. In that moment, I felt so much pain, and I felt so alone. I wanted to cry out to God for comfort, but no words came.

My parents' divorce left me in a lot of pain, but I hadn't let myself deal with it until now. As a freshman in college, I sat alone in a piano practice room on campus, finally allowing myself to let out the pain I had bottled up for years.

In the past, I would ignore the pain rather than allowing myself to work through it. Some people sob their lives away, longing for everyone to sympathize. Some hold back every tear, trying to convince themselves, and those around them, that they are strong. Others are somewhere in-between.

Either way, we all have pain, and we all need to deal with it. We must grieve and then move on.

> "There is a time for everything... a time to weep and a time to laugh, a time to mourn and a time to dance."
>
> Ecclesiastes 3:1,4 (NIV)

As I sat there in the piano room, it was finally my time to choose to move past the fear and work through some inner healing.

I felt completely drained and helpless. With everything within me, I tried to worship Jesus. I was too weak to sing, but he knew I needed his strength, his comfort, his healing touch.

Suddenly I felt my cell phone vibrate. Looking down, I saw my friend Beth's text wondering how I was doing. I responded and within minutes she was sitting next to me on the floor as I cried.

Amid the pain, we can receive Jesus' healing for us and let him mend our broken hearts. This is where the healing begins.

Desensitized

More recently, I was at a high school youth retreat as a leader of six beautiful senior girls. During small group, we talked about their life stories, God's calling on their lives, and any internal walls that might be blocking them in their relationships with God. While I prepared earlier that week, I realized that I too might still have some walls up.

So during the worship service I paused and asked God to show me a wall in my life that was blocking me in my relationship with him. I was expecting to see a long red brick wall representing pride or a thick glass wall representing my judgmental tendencies toward people or something like that. But what God showed me was a surprise.

There was no wall. Rather, I saw myself covered in large metal chains. Chains were wrapped around my arms and legs, crossing behind my back and in front. I struggled to break free, but they were bolted down to the ground and wouldn't budge. I was stuck.

I took a closer look at the chains, trying to understand what God was showing me. I saw the word "pain" on each link. Each metal link represented an experience from my life that hurt and brought me some type of pain that had never fully healed. Each memory of the divorce or of a friend who abandoned me or of a hurtful word that was spoken and never addressed added one more link.

I had gone without letting myself feel for years and hadn't worked through the pain. Throughout high school I hated crying and wouldn't. I'd stop myself. It felt good at the time because I wasn't feeling the pain. Over time my heart hardened as I made myself not feel. I bottled everything up. I was holding onto something that I desperately needed to let go.

Thus, I was becoming desensitized. I was in shackles and didn't even know it. I was bound up and chained down. Not dealing with the pain was desensitizing me and binding me in these emotional chains. I knew it was affecting both my relationship with God and with others. Holding onto this pain was restricting me from moving forward, from loving and being loved.

I needed to break free.

Chain Breaker

A woman was suffering with some medical problems for 12 years. She spent every coin she had in hope that a doctor could find a solution. But nothing was working. Instead of getting better, her condition got worse and worse. Perhaps over those 12 years, she was losing hope and becoming desensitized to the reality of her condition.

Not only was she losing hope and had physical problems, but also due to her sickness, she was a social outcast, dubbed "unclean," and emotionally wrecked. She was utterly broken and needed a holistic healing, inside and out.

But then Jesus entered the picture. She had heard about him. Stories of his supernatural ability to heal the sick spread throughout the village, and for the first time in years the woman felt a flicker of hope. She was desperate for a healing touch.

Large crowds formed around Jesus as he entered their village. The woman pushed her way through the mass of people, reached out and did something totally unacceptable in the culture of that time. She touched him.

Immediately Jesus knew what happened, and rather than condemning her, he reached out to her. His healing power had transferred to her and her life would be forever changed.

> "He said to her, 'Daughter, your faith has healed you. Go in peace and be freed from your suffering."
>
> Mark 5:34 (NIV)

Jesus healed the women, and she was no longer a social outcast. She was free from the chains of suffering that once held her captive. She was finally at peace.

We are healed through the power of Jesus. On the cross he has conquered not only death, but also sin, sickness, destruction, suffering. In the original Greek, the word for salvation not only means salvation, but also deliverance, healing, protection, and wholeness. Jesus died for our healing. His forgiveness on the cross, and in turn as we forgive others, brings deep healing in any area of life: physically, mentally, emotionally, spiritually.

We can cry out and receive this healing, and he will be faithful to answer.

> "Heal me, Lord, and I will be healed; save
> me and I will be saved, for you are the one I
> praise. They keep saying to me, where is
> the word of the Lord? Let it now be
> fulfilled!"

Jeremiah 17:14 (NIV)

We can have full confidence that he will bring us healing; he will save us from these chains of pain.

Jesus' love brings healing and forgiveness breaks us free from the pain. So let it be fulfilled. This is now the season for healing. Let us no longer cry, but laugh. May the power of Christ bind the broken hearted and proclaim freedom for the captives. The night is fleeing and daylight is breaking. The time is now.

In the Garbage

We need to cry. Physically it releases built up tension, emotionally it authenticates our hurt feelings, and spiritually it opens us up to receive the healing power of Jesus. There is a vulnerability that is exposed which allows for emotional surgery to happen on our hearts. That's good. But the healing process doesn't stop there.

Yes, crying helps, but it doesn't fully heal. Off and on during my first couple years at college, I released all the tears that I had bottled up throughout high school. I finally had turned on the nozzle, and boy, did the water flow. But then, after I graduated from college, this pain surfaced again.

My friend had invited me to participate in a small group, and I had been going for six months. This night, part of me wanted to ignore the lingering pain and shut off my emotion; part of me wanted to open my heart up for God's healing. Near the end of the night someone asked me if I was okay. I broke down crying.

That night I went home with a big headache and runny nose. The next morning I woke up sick. I was sick until nine days later when I arrived at the high school youth retreat with my senior girls that I was just telling you about. There I was, at the retreat, finally feeling better and picturing this image of me bound in the chains of pain. I realized I could cry all I wanted to, but until I gave up the role of victim and let go of the pain, I was never going to fully heal.

"All right Jesus, get rid of these chains," I whispered.

Immediately I saw the chains breaking off and falling to the floor. Suddenly I felt like I could breathe easier. But not all the chains had broken off. I asked God for some sort of tool or something so I could finish breaking them off.

He told me to forgive.

I had forgiven the people who had hurt me in the past before, but I needed to do it again. Sometimes we have a hard time forgiving people, so we need to do it a couple times to really let go. I started listing off the family members and friends in my life who came to mind.

"I forgive my dad. I forgive..." I saw more and more

chains break off as I listed more and more people. Finally, all the metal links were lying on the floor. I picked up the chains and threw them in the garbage.

Feel the pain, and then let it go.

Free to Love

> "Drop your chains, sons and daughters.
> Come and run in liberty. We are free … the
> Son has set us free."
>
> "Chainbreaker" by Charlie Hall

Breaking free from the chains of pain opens our hearts to love and be loved.

At the winter youth retreat God had not only revealed to me the chains of pain, but he had broken me free from them. His grace alone broke me free from much of it and then, as I forgave, I reached even more freedom. The chains were gone, and I genuinely noticed a difference.

After spiritually throwing the chains of pain in the garbage and moving on, I felt even more of God's love toward all the students in our group at camp. It was like a rush of compassion. My eyes looked at a student and didn't see their own trash, but only saw their incredible identity and destiny in Christ. My heart felt love for even total strangers.

God had pressed upon my heart a glimpse of his own heart for the people around me. In that moment, God increased my heart for these students, and I do care so much about each one. Seizing the opportunity, I freely prayed over them and spoke truth to them about how God loves them so much.

Even after I returned home, I noticed a difference in myself. Suddenly I genuinely cared about how a friend of mine was doing, even though there had been some issues in our friendship, and I had been apathetic toward her for the past several months. I pulled out my cell phone and sent her a text. A couple days later we got together to catch up and hang out.

And then there's my dad. Yes, I had forgiven him in the past, but there were some things that had never fully healed and as a defense mechanism, I would see whatever my dad did wrong rather than focusing on the right. Thus, over time I came to dislike him in some of those ways so that I had a reason to protect myself from future pain rather than letting myself heal and move on.

After returning from the retreat, I was more understanding of his shortcomings that had hurt me in the past. I wanted to spend time with him. Things weren't suddenly perfect by any means, but I did notice a difference.

When we are healed from the pain, we receive a

> "crown of beauty instead of ashes, the oil of
> gladness instead of mourning, and a
> garment of praise instead of a spirit of
> despair."

Isaiah 61:3 (NIV)

When someone was in mourning during the times of

Isaiah, they would cover themselves in ashes as an outward expression of their inward devastation. Rather than a pauper sitting deprived in the ashes, we are royalty, the beautiful children of the King of Kings!

Jesus takes away the despair and fills us with joy. He breaks the chains off us and saves us. There is healing and freedom, hope and a renewed sense of joy. And through it all we can still sing, "Blessed be the name of the Lord, blessed be your name."

Questions to Explore

- Clear your mind and ask God to show you what walls you have up. What do you see?
- Now ask for Jesus to give you a tool to break down the wall. Do you have the tool? Now tear down that wall until it's destroyed completely. Pick up the pieces and throw them into the garbage.
- Is there anyone who you need to forgive? How would it feel to forgive and let things go?

9 MIND GAMES

This is not a game. It's real. It's like a dream within a dream within reality. The truth and the lies collide. Words play back and forth in your head. Each word echoes in a voice that sounds so familiar. It's one you hear every day when you speak. Yet not every word is yours.

It's like a war of the word. It's a vivid real struggle between ideas that seem to be neither black nor white. The truth and the lies seem to mix into a blended gray. The good doesn't always seem good, and the bad doesn't always seem bad. Yet it's this conniving strategy that puts us in limbo.

Think of the movie *Inception*. It was a continual invasion into the very thoughts of the victim, tricking them into believing things they would normally disbelieve. And if they remained in the dream for too long, they could easily lose focus of the reality. What was true? What was an illusion, a lie?

I shivered, but didn't care. Tears ran down my face. I was furious. It was a cold night, and I was sitting in the driver's seat of my car.

"You're totally worthless. Unimportant. They don't really care about you." These words echoed inside my mind over and over. I gripped the steering wheel tighter and tighter. I knew these things weren't true. Or were they? They felt so real, and I was beginning to believe them.

"No! That is not true! You are completely irreplaceable and loved." But those words of encouragement seemed to get lost among the lies.

"They left you behind. They abandoned you. You're invisible." More thoughts flooded my mind. I felt overpowered by them, and I let them continue. I was too weak to tell them to go away.

As I sat there, being abused by the harsh lies in my head, I talked to God about it. These things weren't true. The Bible says they were lies, yet the piercing thoughts still hurt.

Each lie was coming from Satan and detracted the truth of whom God created me to be. Satan floods our minds with lies. Stop and think about it. Think about the different ideas that pop in and out of your head. Sure, a lot of them are your own thoughts, but many of them are either encouraging truth given by our loving God or depressible lies planted by the devil.

He finds our weak points and fills our minds with lies. For me, the lie that I struggled with the most was that I was messed up because of my parents' divorce. I was messed up.

Divorce leaves our minds vulnerable to Satan's attacks. Because of the pain from the breakup of my family, I was fearful of ending up divorced myself. I had built up walls to protect myself from future pain within any relationship. I recognized that I had many issues that I needed to deal with, and consequently believed that these issues made me messed up. I felt like a burden to others. I felt unlovable and unimportant.

Why else would I have felt abandoned by others in the past? Why else would I have been rejected? The questions and thoughts that plagued my mind were starting to get the best of me.

Battlefield of the Mind

One day, the summer after my freshman year in college, I walked through my dad's bedroom while he was at work, and again I was bombarded with these thoughts: "You're messed up because of the divorce."

I held my head in my hands, wanting these deadly thoughts to leave. Yet, at the same time they were seductive. They were addictive. I almost wanted to hear and believe them.

"But it's not true!" My mind went back and forth, first believing the lie and then the truth ... and then the lie again. It was like a ping pong match. It was as if Satan was shooting flaming arrows at my head, and I didn't know whether to duck and cover or warm my hands by the fire.

This is the battlefield of the mind, a constant war zone of our greatest enemy. Satan actively attacks our minds with lies. When we think of war, we usually think of the army or other branches of the military, but in reality, the greatest war is in the spiritual between forces of good and evil. There is so much going on in the unseen. Ephesians 6:12 explains, "For our struggle is not against flesh and blood, but ... against the powers of this dark world and against the spiritual forces of evil in the heavenly realms."

This is no game. This is very real. Stealthily, the devil sneaks subtle thoughts into our minds that seem harmless at first, like little white lies, but then grow into a monster. He cleverly makes us think we are someone we aren't. He convinces us that we aren't loved, we aren't worthy of love, and that we hold little to no significance. Lies!

We are in a spiritual war, and some of Satan's greatest weapons against us are the lies that he plants in our minds. That's why Romans 12:2 teaches us to "renew our minds" and Hebrews 3:13 tells us to, "encourage one another daily, as long as it is called 'Today,' so that none of you may be hardened by sin's deceitfulness." We need to be aware of our thoughts.

But see, the worst part is that we don't even realize what's happening. We deny it or shrug it off as no big deal. There's not really a war going on in my mind. I'm just indecisive. Or I just don't want to be prideful, and think I'm beautiful or good at something. But the truth is, you are. It's prideful to say that you're not. You are so loved and have been created in the very image of our Creator. He has made you incredible and has generously given you many talents and abilities. And he has established passions within you and has called you to a life of great purpose. Radically living out the destiny God has for us is the very thing Satan tries so desperately to stop.

This battle within the mind happens to all of us. Yes. We are at war. But we must choose what we will do with the lies. That's the most crucial part: deciding whether to believe the lies or not. Yes, it's a battle, but what side will you choose? The truth? Or the lies?

The Truth Is ...

The truth is we are more than conquerors in Christ Jesus. The battle is before us, and we can be victorious. God has won the war. That doesn't mean it will be easy, but it does mean we can stand firm, and we can overcome.

> "Finally, be strong in the Lord and in his mighty power. Put on the full armor of God, so that you can take your stand against the devil's schemes."

> Ephesians 6:10-11 (NIV)

We can be equipped to stand our ground and not be taken out by these lies. In Ephesians, Paul gives a list of spiritual armor: the belt of truth, breastplate of righteousness, shoes of peace, shield of faith, helmet of salvation, and the sword of the spirit.

I understood what most of those meant, but for a while, I didn't quite understand the helmet of salvation. Yet, I think that one may have been the most crucial piece in these mind games I was stuck in. But then one day it clicked.

The helmet is an allusion to Isaiah 59 where the Lord is figuratively dressed in armor with the helmet representing deliverance.

> "... And his desire to deliver is like a helmet on his head ..."

> Isaiah 59:17 (NET)

The helmet of salvation in Ephesians is referring to the deliverance that comes because of Jesus' death and resurrection. This is deliverance from sin and the attacks of Satan.

Jesus overcame Satan on the cross. He overcame sin and death. He overcame evil. He overcame the lies. Truth prevailed.

But not only is the helmet to represent that Christ delivers our minds, but it also reveals that salvation and deliverance involves a thought-out decision, a mental choice. It is our decision whether to be vindicated from these lies or not, and walk in the truth. When Jesus conquered the grave, he gave us full authority so that I didn't have to give in to these lies and let them steer my life. I could live in the freedom of the truth.

What is the lie that can't seem to get out of your head? Now, what is the truth?

The truth is it's not your fault. The truth is you're not alone. You are not worthless. You are important and loved. The truth is I'm not messed up because of my parent's divorce. You are not messed up. The truth is our identity and future is not based on the past, but based on God's grace. The truth is those lies plaguing your mind are not true.

Lie, truth, lie, truth. Back and forth. I was literally pacing back and forth in my dad's bedroom. I had to decide. What would I believe? It seemed so much easier to give in to the lie, but I knew it wasn't true, and believing it would make my life miserable.

I stopped pacing. I took a deep breath and finally decided. I was not "messed up." I decided I would stick with that decision no matter what. Even if it got harder, I was going to stand in the truth that I was not messed up because of my parents' divorce.

Standing in my dad's bedroom, alone in the house, I literally shouted at Satan, "I am not messed up!"

Stand Firm

> "Therefore put on the full armor of God, so
> that when the day of evil comes, you may
> be able to stand your ground, and after you
> have done everything, to stand."

> Ephesians 6:13 (NIV)

Reject the lies of the enemy and stand firm.
The Greek word for "stand firm" is used 158 times

throughout the New Testament: clearly an important idea. It means to fix, to establish, to uphold the authority, to stand immovable like the foundation of a building, to be of an unwavering mind, to remain unharmed, and to stand firm. We have the authority given to us by Jesus to remain unwavering by the attacks of Satan. His lies will not prevail. They will be rendered completely useless.

I engaged in this battle of the mind for an entire week. Every day I paced back and forth, rejecting the lies that bombarded my mind and declaring the truth. At points, I was literally yelling at Satan, proclaiming the truth about who I was. At first, I didn't necessarily believe the truth, but there was something about actually speaking the truth out loud that made me stronger.

Remember how I had been sitting in my parked car on my college campus, shivering in the cold one night? Well, no one was around, and I was angry because of the issues that had come up and the lies that were filling my mind.

But, I realized the problems weren't so much about the people or situation; the problem was Satan's attacks on my life. I was furious. And right there, sitting in my car, I yelled at Satan, telling him to get away from me, or something like that. Suddenly I felt better. A weight was lifted. The true source of the problem had been acknowledged and dealt with. He had no authority in my life, and I was not going to listen to his lies.

Standing in my dad's bedroom, fighting those lies with God's truth, I claimed victory. It was a daily process of forcing my mind to believe the truth. By the end of the week, the lies had died down. They could no longer fight against the power of the truth. The mind games about whether I was messed up or not were finally over. Truth had prevailed.

You Are

I had won the ping pong match.

> "In all these things we are more than conquerors through him who loves us."

Romans 8:37 (NIV)

It wasn't easy persevering through the mind games. And once you've defeated one battle, another will probably pop up sooner or later, but the more you stand firm, the easier it will become to stand firm.

It's like food. If you get in the habit of eating junk food, healthy food doesn't taste very good. And as you start eating the healthy food while rejecting the junk food, it's very difficult because your body craves the junk. But as you persevere, a shift takes place where you no longer crave the junk food; instead you're even repulsed by it. The healthy food now looks appealing, and as you consume more of it, you notice a difference. You feel and look better. You have more energy, and your body is far healthier.

Letting go of the junk was difficult, but the goodness of the truth made me stronger. I felt a lot better about others and myself. I had more passion and energy in life. I was no longer imprisoned by the debilitating thoughts that I was "messed up." I didn't feel as much of a burden to other people anymore. I started feeling more lovable and significant. I am beautiful; I do have value.

You are beautiful; You are incredible. You have greater strength than you realize. Your talents, your passions, your personality; it's all unique and distinctly you. You have great purpose in life to make a powerful impact on the world around you. You are captivating and worth so much more than you think. Remember that.

Claim victory whenever Satan sideswipes you with mind games, temptation and lies about who you are. You can fight and overcome. And you can take a stand to encourage others as they fight. In this truth, there is freedom. Truth prevails.

Questions to Explore

- What is the lie that can't seem to get out of your head?
- On the flipside, what is the truth?
- Now go ahead and yell. There's something powerful about audibly speaking words of truth. Seriously, go find a place where you're alone so you don't feel completely awkward, and shout out the truth at the top of your lungs!

10 DOING LIFE

My junior year in college I ended up living in the freshman girl's dorm. I was in a one-person room at the end of the floor, sharing a bathroom with one other upperclassman. Part of me was excited to live there because that dorm was known for its community, but the other part of me was ashamed.

You see, the year before I was living the good life. As a sophomore, I had gotten into the apartment style housing on campus, a rare feat. I was rooming with four other girls, including two of my best friends, while enjoying the A/C, kitchen, and two large picture windows overlooking the pond and stream that wove its way through campus. I came and went as I pleased, going to class and all sorts of different events, taking in the full college experience.

What I didn't realize until it was too late was that I was living with people, but not really living *with* them. I slept in the same room, but I wasn't doing life together with them. Instead, I was usually out being a social butterfly. And when I was in, I didn't make much effort to build relationships with them.

Nor did I share responsibilities. Since I didn't really use the kitchen, it never occurred to me to clean it or take out the trash. I made sure my desk wasn't too messy and my things stayed confined to my specific space. My mindset was to be responsible for me and me alone. I was completely independent.

Independence. As Americans, we are proud of that word. But when it comes to relationships, it's not so good. Codependence means that someone is completely reliant on someone else to an unhealthy level. Independence is the opposite. Someone doesn't rely on anyone for anything to an unhealthy level. Both are not good. Rather, we should be interdependent: mutually relying on one another and helping each other out.

But because of the divorce, I didn't understand that anymore. To get through the divorce, I had to become totally self-reliant and independent. My parents stopped giving me chores, so I just took care of what was mine, and that's it. They also no longer had any rules for me. If I went out, I may have told my mom or dad that I was leaving, but most of the time they didn't care when I would get back or where I was going. They said I was responsible, and they trusted me. From my perspective, I was on my own and had to fend for myself.

There was no longer much of a family element to living. My view of community became distorted. Since family is where we learn how to live in community, when the family is broken down, we must learn or relearn how to live in community and how to give and receive love.

Near the end of sophomore year, my roommates and I sat down to talk about living arrangements for the following year. I thought everything was fine, and I was excited about living with them again. But then they broke the news. They didn't want to live with me anymore.

Wow. Fist to the stomach. That hurt. They didn't want me as a roommate. I had been the one who originally connected everyone so we could get into the apartment style housing. Now they were kicking me out, and perhaps rightfully so, I admit, since I wasn't very good about doing life together with them.

So the following year, junior year, I was in a cramped little room where I had to walk across the hallway to get to the bathroom, surrounded by loud and crazy freshman girls who would run up and down the hallways screaming at 1am while I was trying to get some sleep. But what I didn't realize was that God was going to orchestrate things so that I would meet someone who would help me understand what living in community really meant.

Unworthy

As a requirement for my degree in youth ministry, I needed to complete an internship during the summer before my senior year of college. For months, I was searching out different opportunities and asking around for suggestions. My new friend Rebecca, a freshman who lived two rooms down from me, enthusiastically suggested I spend the summer with her family in Colorado Springs and fulfill my internship at her church's youth group. It sounded like fun so I did my research and continued talking with her about the possibility.

Her parents offered to open their home to me, free of charge, for three whole months. I would become part of their family, venturing out on camping trips and running errands and sitting down to dinner, all of which I hadn't done with my own family in more than ten years. Soon the idea of living with her family in Colorado Springs for the summer became very exciting.

One night I wrote a journal entry to God:

> Daddy, I don't know what to say. I'm blown away. Going to Colorado means being a part of a healthy family for three months. I will be able to see what a godly family is supposed to look like and learn how to cook and whatever else. I haven't sat down as a family for dinner since fifth grade. And now I'm tearing up thinking about it. Yet, I also fear abandonment. I fear either becoming too attached, leaving and never seeing them again, or I don't know, something happening while I'm there. It will take trust and hope. I fear being a part of the family, but also not being part of the family. Daddy, if this is as good as this sounds, I don't deserve it. I want it, but I don't feel like I'm worth it. Wow. I didn't

think I'd ever say that.

We tend to have distorted views of ourselves, not feeling like we are worth enough to be loved by the people around us. I was completely overwhelmed and didn't feel like I deserved such an amazing blessing. I didn't feel like I was worth being loved by her family. I felt very nervous and even scared. I didn't want to be an inconvenience. But I knew these feelings I had about my identity weren't true – all these fears were lies. At that moment, I realized this experience with Rebecca's family was exactly how God wanted to bless me.

Now it was clear exactly what my internship was supposed to be for the summer. Instead of choosing to go to El Salvador to work with a mission's organization, or a little town in the north woods of Wisconsin to work with a very small youth group, or California to work with a mega church, I chose a church I knew very little about in the foothills of Colorado.

Why? Because I needed to experience God's love through a family who didn't even know me. I needed to discover how wide and long and high and deep God's love is for me as well as how valuable, treasured, and irreplaceable I am. Because I needed to find my worth as God's beautiful creation, cherished daughter, and essential piece to the body of Christ. I didn't feel like I was worth it, but knew I needed to experience it anyway.

Worth It

You are worth being loved and loving others. That's easy

for me to say about you, but what about me? I can look at you and see this amazing person with all sorts of gifts and talents, but when I look in the mirror, I'm not always so captivated. Yet, can I really love others without first loving myself?

"Yes!" you might say. I disagree. Think of how much the way we view ourselves affects the way we treat ourselves and treat others. How can I love someone without giving them the opportunity to love me in return? One of the greatest ways to love someone is to let them love me. But how can I let them love me if I feel unlovable?

You've heard it said, "Love your neighbor as yourself." If you don't love yourself and you're supposed to love others as yourself, then you can't love others. So how can we love others? How can we feel loved so that we can truly love the people around us?

I tend to get caught up in trying to be a good person and love others, but that in of itself doesn't work. It feels like checking the box and not really making a lasting impact. It feels exhausting instead of exhilarating. So instead of stopping to figure out why, we just keep doing more and more.

But then I realized, we're called to love God first and out of that love for God, loving others is natural. What's the greatest commandment? Love God. What's the second? Love others. Jesus even said that when you love someone, you love him.

Okay. But how do I love God? And what does that have to do with loving myself?

We must first be loved by God. When we receive God's love, we can't help but love him in return. And when we're loving him in return, we can't help but love others. But we first must let ourselves be loved by God.

Let me give you an example. Growing up I never considered myself as ugly, but I certainly wouldn't go as far to say that I was beautiful either. I was "eh" and I was content with it. At one point, I started a journal where I would listen to God and write down whatever I felt him say to me. I'd start writing with:

> Dear Caitlyn,
>
> I love you ...

And then I would continue to write as God whispered to my heart. By the way, if you do this, awesome, but remember it usually takes some practice to distinguish God's voice from our own, so make sure what you write is biblical truth.

So I would write this down in my journal and almost every time after the words "I love you" came "You are beautiful." Clearly those words were from God, not me. At first I kind of ignored those three simple words about my alleged beauty, but slowly over time those words he pressed upon my heart were changing me. One day I looked in the mirror and truly thought I was beautiful. It was crazy. God's truth was sinking deep within me, and I was starting to believe it.

Let God's word sink in past your skin to your core. Let his love penetrate your heart. Talk with him. Dance with him. Let him hold you in his arms. Be loved by him. You are worth being loved by him. He created you. You are his priceless creation.

And as you experience his love, it will be completely natural to love others. He loves to love others through you, and he loves to love you through others. You are worth being loved and loving others.

Road Trip

Road trips are hard for me. They're not exactly the most fun journey. I'm not a fan of driving two days straight across farmland. No hills, no people, just an occasional herd of cows.

But finally Rebecca and I arrived in Colorado where the Rockies were the backdrop to her home. The very first thing we did was sit down to eat dinner as a family. I wanted to cry. Then we went to her younger brother's high school swim meet. There, Rebecca's mom introduced me to the other parents as her "daughter for the summer." For three months, I experienced what it was like to live as a part of this family.

It sounds wonderful and it was, but it was also hard. Allowing myself to be loved, even in those simple ways of acceptance and provision, was a real struggle for me. All summer long I was bombarded with all sorts of difficult news about my family back home, and every time Rebecca and her mom were there for me. They took time to get to know me even though I had nothing to give them in return. They didn't have to walk with me through my messy life. They didn't have to love me. There was no reason to. But they did.

Yet even during that, I still tried to earn their love. I still tried to justify it. I still tried to be independent and self-reliant. But they kept loving me anyway. They took me to Pikes Peak and camping out in the mountains. While we were camping, Rebecca took me up to her favorite spot in the world. What an honor to stand beside her, looking out over the beautiful landscape from that sacred spot.

On the hike back down to the campsite, my footing slipped and I fell, sliding across a sheet of rock and landing just shy of the edge of the cliff. Sharp pain shot through my foot and up my leg as I felt fluid rush into my ankle. It swelled up rapidly to two or three times its size. It hurt like crazy! All I could do was pray. Rebecca sat with me, and we prayed for my ankle. After a minute of praying, suddenly my ankle stopped hurting. It was incredible! The pain was completely gone. I had never experienced anything like it before.

Even without pain, my ankle was still super swollen and awkward to walk on. Rebecca called her brother over to be my human crutch, and the three of us worked our way down the mountain. You should have been there. It was rather funny.

I was on crutches for the last couple weeks in Colorado, and had to rely on the family to help me with everything. Yes, God took away the pain from my ankle, but he didn't completely heal it, allowing me the opportunity to learn how to let others take care of me and love me.

Receiving that kind of love is humbling and life changing. It's hard and not the most fun journey to go on. But it's worth it. I was worth it. We must allow ourselves to do life together with others, to be known by and to know others, and to be loved by and to love others.

Community

> I went to Colorado to discover God's radical love. I didn't find it – well, at least not how I expected. I expected God's radical love to be ... loud. But it wasn't. Instead, I experienced his soft, gentle love. It was quiet like a sweet whisper, not loud and booming. And that still love was radical. It changed my life; I will never be the same.

I put my pen down and closed my journal. The car drove through the Black Hills of South Dakota. My mom was at the wheel. My time in Colorado was over, and my mom had graciously flown out to keep me company on the long road trip back.

Honestly, I didn't want to leave. I felt at home there. Yes, there was some conflict that arose at a few points during the summer, but ultimately I felt God's peace and joy. Laughing came so easily. I'd laugh at random little things. And I would randomly burst into song ... usually Christmas songs. I have no idea why. It was kind of weird singing Christmas songs in the middle of the summer, but that's what happened.

I felt whole. I felt alive. I felt loved. Unconditional love within a community that does life together brings wholeness.

I stuck my earbuds in and cranked up the music on my iPod. I didn't want to go back to reality and encounter all the family junk that was going on. Turning away from my mom, I looked out the window and let the tears run silently down my face.

While I was in community with Rebecca's family I felt whole, yet my heart still ached. I had experienced what community was supposed to look like, but now I was returning to my own family, a broken family with broken relationships. Could I somehow experience this community within my own family? Could my relationships with my parents and siblings be restored? Did I even want to bother putting in the effort to rebuild these relationships? Were they worth it?

Questions to Explore

- What do you see when you look in a mirror?
- Describe what you think it means to live in community.
- Write about a time when you felt loved and ask God to show you his love in a new way.

11 REDEFINING HOME

It was a warm, sunny spring day. I was driving a high school student home after eating ice cream while hanging out at the park. She had cotton candy ice cream; I had mint Oreo.

The sunroof was open and the music turned down. We were talking about life. She was telling me about how her parents had gotten divorced when she was little. Ever since the divorce her parents moved around town from one rental house or apartment to the next. And almost every other day she would switch between her mom's and dad's.

I turned the corner and sighed. My heart connected with the deep longing that I knew she had, even if she didn't come right out and say it. I glanced over at her.

"Do you feel like you don't have a place to call home? Like you have different places where you live, but you don't ever feel at home?"

She responded without skipping a beat, admitting that she had never felt at home before, but her mom just bought a house, so maybe that would change. Maybe.

In college, I was finally in a place where I felt at home. The divorce had destroyed my sense of home, but the moment I stepped out of the car onto the campus for the first time, I felt completely at home.

It's hard to describe. I had never been there before, yet it felt like my soul was already connected with the community there. It was a profound feeling that leaves an imprint on your heart. I even remember the exact spot where I was standing when I felt it for the first time.

After the breakdown of my family and losing the house I grew up in, I had rediscovered a new home. My college campus was where I lived and made incredible friends who became like my new family, learned new things, and discovered truths about ourselves. It was where God brought healing and change.

But now my time in college was over. People would come up to me and ask if I was excited about graduating. Of course they expected a hearty yes, but that's not what they got.

Most of my peers were super excited to finally have their hard-earned degree and be free from school forever. Not me. Graduating college was hard. The moment I moved off campus, I lost my home and my family all over again.

Everything within me longed for a place where I felt like I belonged. Everything within me longed for a place to call home. When our sense of home is destroyed by the divorce, it is important to have a place where we belong.

The Question

"I hate hurting ... I wish I had a home. I wish I had love. I wish I understood what love really was. I wish I had some answers. All I have is hope that You will be faithful. Somehow ..."

I reread the words I had written in my journal. I remembered writing those words and wishing Jesus would just come and take me away from this place. I closed the journal and threw it into a box. Once again I was standing in a room with bare walls and boxes cluttering the floor.

Ever since I moved out of the house I grew up in and into the apartment with my mom, I had been on a journey of figuring out what "home" really was. I wasn't about to call my mom's apartment or my dad's townhouse "home." I was always going to "my mom's" or to "my dad's." I was never simply headed "home." I almost felt like I would betray my true childhood home if I called it that.

Moving out of college sent me searching for a new place to call home. Yet the concept of home shouldn't always be moving. Every time you leave one place and go to the next, is "home" redefined? They say, "Home is where the heart is," but what does that mean? Is that even true or just some nice phrase someone came up with? What is home?

I graduated college and went searching for a place where I could feel at home, where I felt like I belonged. I browsed the Internet and asked around, looking at different apartments, but without a roommate to split the rent, I couldn't find anything that I was willing to pay.

In the meantime, I moved back in with my dad, but I hated it. Living with him was hard because we would butt heads too often. Sure, we could have a lot of fun together, but I wanted to live in a place where I felt completely accepted and at peace.

As often as I could, I'd retreat to my grandparents' house. This is one of the few places where I've felt the most at home in the past. It is a cozy one-story house in Wisconsin, not too far from a wonderful frozen custard shop. At Christmas time, all the family would cram into the little house, covering the floors with inflatable mattresses. I'd watch sports on TV with my grandpa, eat the wonderful food and desserts my grandma spoils us with, and play card games late into the night.

Their home is a place of peace, love, and acceptance. I know they are always proud of me and never did I feel judged.

But what about other places? I struggled with this question for years. The changes that take place because of the divorce result in feeling a loss of home. I felt lost, incomplete, and without a place that I felt like I could call home.

I was on a journey of redefining home.

Beyond the Family Tree

I made a little girl cry. We tried to comfort her by telling her my face doesn't really look like this, but she didn't quite get it. Aside from that moment, being a clown was a blast, and I loved being a complete goofball, making a fool out of myself simply for the entertainment of others. It was senior year in high school and I was with my youth group in El Salvador putting on skits, singing and dancing, and telling kids about Jesus.

For ten days, we lived with the locals and despite the language barrier, they soon became like family. The night before our youth group left, we met in a room to worship together and say our goodbyes. We embraced each other one last time, and I couldn't help but cry. These were my brothers and sisters. This was my family. This was my home.

I began to realize that my true family and my true home far exceeded the walls of a house and names on a family tree. Living at college opened my eyes to this idea even more as I continued my journey of redefining home.

The phrase "Home is where the heart is" kept ringing in my ears. It made sense. Where you feel loved and where you feel like you belong is where I would want to call my home. The place where my heart feels full and connected, passionate and alive. It should be a place where I feel at peace and at rest.

Then during one Christmas break in college, I stumbled upon a verse that suddenly made it all click. I was painting ornaments to give as presents to my family and a couple close friends. Slowly I examined the silver ball, thinking about what to paint next. I knew I wanted to paint something having to do with *The Wizard of Oz* because that was my friend's favorite movie.

"There's no place like home." The famous quote came to mind. I turned to my laptop and clicked open a new tab in the browser. She was a Christian friend so I was curious if the Bible had any verse related to that idea. I brought up a search, but wasn't finding anything. I kept looking. I started down a different trail, going back to the idea that home is where the heart is.

After a few more minutes of browsing, I finally stumbled upon 1 John 3:19, which says that we should "...set our hearts at rest in his presence." The idea was so simple, yet it changed everything.

If home is where our heart is and our heart is meant to be in God's presence, then we will feel at home whenever we are in his presence. The first time I entered the church I attended during college, I felt at home. The moment I walked through the doors into the main atrium, I felt a peace settle on me as if I belonged there. It was that feeling that beckoned me to choose that church as my home church where I would attend and serve.

But being in God's presence isn't restricted to the walls of a church building. Feeling at home isn't restricted to the four walls of a house. It goes with you. Your sense of home doesn't have to change every time your address changes or when there's a significant change in your family. Ultimately our family is the family of God, and our home is in the presence of God.

In His Presence

The hotel was a train. Yes, a train. I slept on a tiny top bunk in the very end car of a train that was parked on an old platform. There were two trains and they didn't move; they just sat there. Outside were a few small buildings with freezing cold showers and toilets that flushed in the opposite direction. There were a couple pool tables inside the train station and an empty pool outside at the far end past the trains. That was our hotel.

I was in Africa, a place I never thought I'd ever be. Nor did I think I would be exploring the heart of South Africa in all its financial poverty and cultural riches as well as touring the heavily European influenced city of Cape Town with a couple hundred people from a variety of different nations, nearly all of whom I didn't know. For two weeks, I trained and served alongside of some of the most humble and loving people I've ever met. We were there for the 3rd Lausanne Congress on World Evangelization, originally founded by Billy Graham.

More than 4,000 people from more than 200 different countries all around the world were united under one roof in Cape Town, South Africa to worship God and discuss effective global evangelism. This weeklong event made history. Nothing of this magnitude with so many different ethnicities had ever taken place. It was incredible, and I had the privilege of be a part of it.

While I was in Africa I felt the most amount of love I have ever experienced in my life. There was a constant stream of selfless serving and encouraging among the group. It literally was like heaven on earth.

At one point during the week, right before one of the main sessions, a small group of people invited me to join them as they prayed in the hallway just outside the plenary hall. They passionately asked God to move and work in a powerful way that week. Then they shifted over to praying for each other. They circled around me, and began encouraging me and speaking truth into my life.

A girl about my age leaned in closer and began to speak into my ear so I could clearly hear her above the noise of the crowd around us. I could tell these words were not her own; God was giving her specific words for me personally. "Be at home in his presence," she said. I was completely taken aback.

"Be at home in his presence." She had no idea the questions that had plagued my mind about what home was. She probably didn't even know my name. Yet God used her to confirm the incredible truth he had already been teaching me. In a place where I felt immersed in his love and deeply encouraged by so many brothers and sisters in Christ, God finally brought me to a new place, a place within my own heart, where I felt completely at home.

No matter where we are, we can enjoy the family around us and rest in God's presence.

One Last Question

Not long after I moved back to my dad's townhouse post-college, a friend invited me to share an apartment with her. I lived there for about a year but now it was time to move again. Soon I'd be packing, surrounded by boxes and white walls. I'd leave and head to ... well, I wasn't sure where I'd be moving to yet, but that was okay.

This time I didn't feel a lost sense of home. I felt like pretty much wherever I went I would have the capacity to feel at home. It doesn't matter where I am or how often I move. Home doesn't change with every season. Home can be a constant, as constant as God's faithfulness.

And I've seen his faithfulness. Over these past ten or so years of my journey I have seen him walk with me through all the hard times, picking me up and placing me on my feet even when I just wanted to lie in bed and not move. He has broken me free from pain and fear. He has brought me healing, emotionally and physically. He has been there every step of the way and he will continue to be there.

Have you ever experienced that kind of peace and hominess in God's presence? It is a place of contentment, not of judgment, belonging, not condemnation. God's presence is a place of acceptance and constant friendship.

No matter where we go in life, he is there. He is with us and will take good care of us, continually filling our lives with the people who love us. We are surrounded by a kind of family everywhere we go. We are never alone. No matter what we go through, even after going through the divorce, we are still so loved; there will always be a place where we belong.

Yet, I still had one last question that bothered me. If I can feel at home no matter where I am and ultimately my family is far greater than my own blood relatives, do my family, my parents and siblings and relatives, really matter? Do I have to put up with these broken relationships? I mean, for the most part I liked my individual relationships with most of my family members, but my family as a unit was still quite dysfunctional. Sometimes family gatherings would still turn into complete disasters. Couldn't I just disown them? It seemed to be a lot easier ...

Would it be possible to feel this same sense of home within my own family? Could my relationships with my parents and siblings be truly restored? If so, did I even want to bother putting in the effort to rebuild these relationships? Were they worth it?

Questions to Explore

- Did you have a stable childhood home, or did you move around a lot and never really feel planted? How did your situation make you feel?
- Where do you feel like you belong? Why?
- Have you ever felt at home and at peace in God's presence? Write down where you were and how you felt.

12 FAMILY REBUILDING

The lady ushered us single file through hallways cluttered with old-time photographs to the back of the house. We entered the large studio room with a huge backdrop draped down from the ceiling, covering the entire expanse of one wall. I looked around the corner into a long, narrow closet. It was filled with all sorts of cowboy costumes, stuffed animals, and a variety of other props.

It was my grandparents' 50th anniversary. The entire family on my mom's side, all 14 of us, had piled into several cars and headed toward the small town of Rio where my grandma grew up. My little cousin and I squeezed into my mom's tiny, sporty blue car with a fun little swoosh detail on the sides.

We drove through the cornfields of Wisconsin until we pulled up outside a quaint house that had been converted into a photo studio where we would take a family portrait.

In front of the portrait backdrop was an odd collection of chairs and stools ranging in height. After the photographer made a few quick adjustments, she began positioning each family member by pairing us up. Of course she started with my grandparents: front and center. Next up was my brother Chris and his wife, Sarah. They sat on low crates just to the left. Then she directed my uncle and aunt to sit on high stools to the right.

The photographer continued to organize our family, guessing who was coupled with whom. I'm sure my uncles made a few wise cracks. Finally only my mom and I remained. She paired up mother and daughter and stuck us in the back.

Now the family portrait hangs over the couch in my grandparents' family room. Whenever I glance up at it I see a happy family. I love this group of people. We know how to laugh, have fun, and enjoy life. There's little drama and quite a bit of genuine caring for one another.

Yet, when I look at the portrait I also see the missing faces. If it weren't for the divorce, my dad would have been standing in the picture too. It's like our family loses people, but it also gains people. According to my brother, my sister-in-law, Sarah, was our "photo beautification project." And now, several years later, we have more wonderful new additions to the family: my nieces and nephews, and of course, my brilliant husband Dennis and our adorable son Samuel.

It's said that people come and go, but family stays forever. Is that true? Can we simply let our family portrait continue to change over the years, whether it's for the good or the bad? Is there an invisible bond that somehow ties these people in this photo together or is a complete picture something for which we must fight?

Even though our sense of community reaches much farther than our family tree, our family is incredibly important. Divorce breaks down families and creates a lot of broken and even dysfunctional relationships. However, those people and those relationships are still beautiful and significant. Choosing to invest in family relationships is difficult, but important.

Disowned

Honestly, this was the most difficult chapter for me to write, which is why I left it for last. Because truthfully, I didn't like my family. Sometimes I felt judged, inferior, or inadequate. Sometimes I felt boxed in by bickering, arguing, and conflict. Family gatherings were not exactly my favorite things to attend.

In fact, when Sarah's baby shower fell on a Sunday at the same time as youth group, I absolutely did not want to go. I didn't want to give up my favorite thing of the week to be at another potentially painful or awkward family event. It turned out to be a lot of fun, yet part of me still would have preferred hanging out with all my high school sisters in my small group at church.

But I chose to go to the baby shower, because deep inside I knew my family was supposed to be important, and I wanted to show that to all the girls I was mentoring. It made me sad that I felt that way about my family. Yet it was true. I didn't really feel like my family was all that important. The divorce had taught me it wasn't.

Truthfully, at that time, I just wanted to disown them all. It would have been easier not to acknowledge my family than to try to repair the brokenness and to hope that I could enjoy spending time with them again, like I once did during my childhood. It was easier to move out of my dad's townhouse into an apartment than deal with the misunderstandings, conflict, and harbored pain. My sister Carolyn was living all the way out on the west coast so why should I bother trying to connect with her when she was so far away? Chris and his family lived closer, but even that didn't seem that important.

I also began to question the significance of Jesus. If we're saved by grace, and even Abraham was saved by grace as Hebrews 11 talks about, what is the need for Jesus? Abraham didn't have Jesus. So why did he matter?

During my questioning, someone pointed out to me that our view of God the Father tends to be impacted by our view of our dads. Similarly, our view of our moms influences our view of the Holy Spirit. And what stood out the most to me was that our view of our siblings changes our view of Jesus. Suddenly it all made sense.

Yes, of course, Jesus was important! He changed everything. He's truth and forgiveness. Apart from him we are totally screwed up. Jesus was God's greatest display of love, sacrifice, and his presence with us. Jesus supersedes time, and his grace covers the past, present, and future. It is because of that grace Abraham was saved. God longs to be close with us. He longs for reconciliation between him and us. Jesus was willing to do absolutely anything needed to restore our relationship with him.

I began to think, perhaps my siblings were also important. Perhaps my relationship with my dad was important. Maybe everyone in my family held great significance in my life and deserved a chance for reconciliation. Perhaps fighting to restore my family relationships was worth it. Maybe *they* were worth it. Maybe I was worth it … or maybe not. I still wasn't so sure. After a divorce, family relationships are broken, and we may not want to mend them.

Not So Bad

I watched Sarah strap my baby niece snuggly into her car seat. She contently bounced up and down, munching on her teething rubber giraffe named Sophie.

"Good bye, Evie," I gently shook her little foot.

Sarah and I hugged, and she climbed into the driver's seat. I leaned against the car and looked through the open window.

"Sarah, I have a random, well I guess not that random … Anyway, I have a question for you."

"Is it about birth control?" She asked in a low voice.

"No!" I laughed.

I looked down and shifted my weight from one foot to the other. I felt awkward asking her my question, but I needed to know the answer.

"Um …" I paused, trying to gain the confidence to ask my question. Sarah is one of my favorite people. When she and my brother started dating, I made a point to give her a hard time to make sure she was okay for my brother. Yes, I was the classic protective younger sister. For her first Christmas present, rather than giving Sarah a legit gift, I gave her a random picture I took of a lemur. Yet somehow she actually loved it.

Over time this became a fun inside joke. One year for Christmas, she gave me a certificate stating that I had adopted a lemur. My perception of Sarah went from skeptical to admiration. And I wondered what her perception of my family was. I didn't like my family, but I didn't choose my family so I was stuck with them. Sarah, however, chose my brother and in doing so, she also chose my family.

"Um ... Do you like my family?" I went on to explain what I meant. She smiled.

Her response went something like, "Sure there are some issues in your family, but all families have that. Of course I like your family."

Just by how she interacted with my family, Sarah helped me like my family again, opening my eyes to the good side of my family. Perhaps my family wasn't all that bad after all.

How we view our family relationships is crucial, and my perspective had to encompass not only the bad but also more importantly the good. When I was a little kid, I only saw the good in my family and not the bad. This view flip-flopped after the divorce. I no longer really saw much of the good, but mostly only the bad. And just as we can't wear those masks and ignore the bad, we can't ignore the good in a family either. There's a reason for the smiles in a family portrait.

Maybe the good that I had ignored was enough to validate a difficult journey into rebuilding relationships with my family members after all. They were worth it. I was worth it. These relationships, though once broken and shattered, were itching to be put back together. The healing process needed to be continued. Love needed to prevail. Family relationships are worth reconciling.

The Other Side

I have a confession to make. I have taken my dad for granted. There were times that all I could see were his glaring flaws. I seemed to ignore all the incredible ways he has faithfully showed his love to me.

My dad loves to laugh, goof around, and have fun with me. He'd put food in my belly, a roof over my head, and always paid for my insurance and phone bills. In the past, sometimes I'd feel judged or as if I didn't meet his expectations, yet he often tells me how proud he is of me. He encourages me to follow my dreams, listens to me, and gives advice when I ask.

I get my sense of adventure and creativity from my dad. We always choose to do things differently, using clever ways to get a job done. I also admire his perseverance. A lot of times he feels stuck in life, but he always pushes through. He doesn't let present failures stop him from accomplishing future successes.

After I'd been dating Dennis, the incredible servant-hearted man of God who is now my husband, he heard the song *Cinderella* by Steven Curtis Chapman. Dennis sent me a text because it reminded him of me. I asked him why since I was never big into princesses while growing up.

Dennis told me the song reflected my dad and me. It's a story of a dad singing about dancing with his daughter and cherishing every moment with her before she grew up. Dennis mentioned to me how he liked my dad and loved how well he and I got along. I was surprised. I didn't think my dad and I got along that well at all.

But Dennis was right. My dad really does care about me. So Dad, thank you. Thank you for all the laughs and fun times. Thank you for all the sacrifices you have made for me, especially the ones about which I know I'm completely clueless. I appreciate you, respect you, and love you. I am blessed.

And Mom, I thank you for your love and grace. I cherish that I can talk with you about anything without ever feeling judged, and you give sound advice.

Thank you, Carolyn, for putting up with your self-righteous and judgmental little sister. I appreciate how much you care about me. I love you and am so grateful for you.

Chris, I respect you and look up to you. I'm proud to have you as my brother.

Sarah, thank you for helping me see the good in my family again.

Dennis, thank you for helping me understand and appreciate my dad.

And to all my family, my aunts and uncles, cousins,

and grandparents, you are all absolutely wonderful, and I genuinely enjoy my relationships with all of you. We have been through a lot of hard times together, but we have made it. And as we continue to go through struggles, let us unite and push through it together. This family is important and such a blessing, each one of you. You are all loved, and you all matter.

Be thankful for the family that you do have. It has taken me years and years of healing from the divorce to be able to finally say that I am genuinely thankful. The family that I once wanted to disown now is deeply important to me. It takes time. It took me months before I could finally finish writing this chapter. But the journey of learning to be grateful is worth it.

Just the Beginning

I found a picture. Not just any picture, but a picture of my old house. Or should I say my old home. This was the place where countless memories were made.

Yet over time, things change. Days pass. There are good days; there are bad. Smiley faces, sad faces. People come and go. The wind blows. Summer turns to fall; spring still comes after the long, cold winter. Life happens.

My house, which was once the white one with blue shutters, now was painted an ugly puke green. The beautiful steep roof was raised so it was almost flat.

The big backyard, where we used to jump in giant piles of leaves, build snowmen, and play catch, was now surrounded by a red cast-iron fence.

Every day riding the bus back to my mom's apartment during high school, we would drive right past the house. Every day I watched it slowly change as the new family remodeled it. We see our lives change around us over time, but it's our decision what we choose to do with that change.

I finally chose to accept the divorce and receive support from a close group of friends. I made the decision to hold onto my hope and persevere through the pain. And I decided not to let society's labels haunt me, but rather give God complete control.

Healing doesn't happen overnight. It's a journey; it's a choice whether to break free from the fear, forgive amid pain, and fight the lies. This is my story. This has been my struggle to love and be loved. But this is also my victory. This is God's faithfulness.

No matter what happens, there is hope. And no matter what, you are loved. No matter what path you take, no matter what choices you make, God will always love you and freely extend his grace to you. His arms are open wide, and you can feel at home in his presence. As you trust him, God will transform your story of pain into one of hope. Your story matters. You matter.

I chose this journey. I didn't choose the divorce. I didn't want my family to be broken, and God has brought me healing through all the questions and pain. He has turned all of this for good, and I choose not to let it all go in vain.

Earlier I shared with you my prayer to Jesus back in junior high. I prayed that if my parents got a divorce that at least one person would be saved because of it. I prayed that God would turn all the bad for the good and use my experience to touch at least one life. Not only has he done that, but perhaps he will continue to use this story to bring people hope. God can do immeasurably more than all we could ask or imagine. And this is certainly not the end of my story.

What about you? What will you choose? Will you continue this journey of healing and put your trust in Jesus to transform your life? Will you let your story be in vain or will you reach out and encourage others?

You have so much to offer the people around you. The comfort and hope you can receive from God can also be shared. There's a hurting world out there in desperate need of love, and you can make a difference.

How will your story end?

Questions to Explore

- What are your family relationships like?
- List the good that you see in your family.
- What's next? Will you continue this journey and encourage others to do the same?

ABOUT THE AUTHOR

Caitlyn Neel earned her degree in Youth Ministry and Adolescent Studies at Judson University. She has spent the past decade mentoring students and speaking to youth groups all across the country. Caitlyn is a proud mom of the cutest toddler in the world and a wife to a brilliant engineer.

MAR   2018